ASSESSING HISTORICAL THINKING AND UNDERSTANDING

Assessing Historical Thinking and Understanding advocates for a fundamental change in how educators think about making sense of learners' developing cognition and understanding in history. Author Bruce VanSledright argues that traditional and typical standardized testing approaches are seldom up to the task of measuring the more complex understandings students are asked to attain, as they cannot fully assess what the student knows. As an alternative, he points forward along a path toward changes in learning, teaching, and assessing that closely aligns with the Common Core State Standards. He delves into the types of history knowledge the standards require, illustrates how they can be applied in-use in history learning contexts, and theorizes how the standards might fit together cognitively to produce deep historical understandings among students in teaching-learning contexts. By providing a variety of assessment strategies and items that align with the standards, and identifying rich, useful assessment rubrics applicable to the different types of assessments, he offers an important resource for social studies teachers and curriculum writers alike.

Bruce VanSledright is Professor of History and Social Studies Education at the University of North Carolina, Charlotte, USA.

ASSESSING HISTORICAL THINKING AND UNDERSTANDING

Innovative Designs for New Standards

Bruce A. VanSledright

Routledge
Taylor & Francis Group

NEW YORK AND LONDON

First published 2014
by Routledge
711 Third Avenue, New York, NY 10017

Simultaneously published in the UK
by Routledge
2 Park Square, Milton Park, Abingdon, Oxon OX14 4RN

Routledge is an imprint of the Taylor & Francis Group, an Informa business

© 2014 Taylor & Francis

The right of Bruce A. VanSledright to be identified as author of this work
has been asserted by him in accordance with sections 77 and 78 of the
Copyright, Designs and Patents Act 1988.

Library of Congress Cataloging-in-Publication Data

A catalog record has been requested for this book.

ISBN: 978-0-415-83697-5 (hbk)
ISBN: 978-0-415-83698-2 (pbk)
ISBN: 978-0-203-46463-2 (ebk)

Typeset in Bembo
by Apex CoVantage, LLC

CONTENTS

PREFACE

In the book *The Challenge of Rethinking History Education*, I attempted to lay out an approach to teaching history that was quite different than what we have typically done in the past. Much more familiar to most of us is the approach in which the history teacher, as sage on the stage who is following the mandated U.S. history curriculum trajectory, narrates a continuous story of nation-building progress from early British exploration and colonization of North America, to the development of an independent nation, and on through the centuries to 21st-century global dominance. Students operate largely as passive recipients of that storyline and are expected to reproduce it on command.

By contrast, I suggested an approach rooted in research studies on how students learn history that put those students into investigative roles. Instead of listening to a story already complete, students would investigate the sources of the stories we often tell with the goal of constructing their own interpretations and understandings. They would become apprentices in what it means *to do history in order to come to understand the American past more deeply*. The history teacher, in my conception, moves into the role of more knowledgeable other, expert guide, and apprenticeship facilitator, one who creates clear investigative rules, watches intensely, and joins the process as often as necessary in order to help students learn to think historically and thereby produce their best work.

To date, and somewhat to my surprise, the most controversial aspect of that book has not been its different approach, the act of redefining curriculum, teacher, and student roles, but rather the chapter in the book on assessment. In developing that chapter, I had assumed that redefined roles necessitated redefined assessment approaches, consequently bringing improved overall coherence to what I was proposing. If learning were reframed, then how teachers assess that learning also needed to be reframed, or so I reasoned. To that end, I devoted considerable time to introducing and explaining the idea of using weighted multiple-choice items (WMCs) as a replacement for the traditional single-correct-answer multiple-choice items with which we are so familiar. I offered a cluster of examples and showed how my history teacher protagonist, Mr. Becker, went about employing them. I also provided weighting structure principles and rationales for the items he designed and used.

Among prospective and practicing teachers and social studies school district supervisors I have worked with and talked to following the book's publication, these items could hardly have produced more questions and general consternation. Both groups have been troubled by them. How could there be three possible acceptable options and only one wrong one? Wasn't that upside down? How could that work? What did I mean by the best response receiving 4 points, a second best receiving 2 points, a third being awarded 1 point, and the last option being the only one to get 0 points because it was wrong? Say what? And how in the world would you grade a test that contained, say, 10 such items in which the top score would be 40 points, and even 10 points out of 40 (or the equivalent of 25% of the maximum score) for someone choosing all 1-point options, for example, would still technically not be failing?

None of this made much sense to them, despite the fact that I was arguing for an easily administered set of items that, it appeared to me, produced powerful diagnostic evidence of student learning capabilities in history, if they were used as designed. This evidence, I reasoned, could be deployed to make adjustments to pedagogical approaches because it was closely aligned with the nature of history as a disciplinary practice and to the investigative orientation of the learning approach I was suggesting. I had imagined that the approach and item design would be widely embraced, perhaps even immediately. I was wrong.

As I thought back on the questions teachers and supervisors were asking and the general angst that my assessment design generated, I began to realize that the questions were born of understandable tensions. The practice of testing as a vehicle for sorting, stratifying, and selecting out students has deep roots in American education, and in many ways it drives the now deeply entrenched and taken-for-granted educational accountability movement. The assessment approach I was recommending, with its stress on learning and diagnosing its progress, did not dovetail particularly well with that practice because its principles operated from different assumptions about the purposes for assessing students.

This book is an effort to address those teachers' and supervisors' many questions. In it, I describe the rather sharp limitations of common testing approaches; point out how the designs I offer assume a different role for assessment that is more applicable to the classroom work of history teachers; and expand on the examples, principles, and theories that underpin my arguments. As I have done before, I root all of this in a research-based model of learning in history. I also attempt to show how what I am proposing aligns closely with elements of the English/Language Arts Common Core Standards and the social studies state inquiry framework. Consequently, it points forward along a path toward changes in learning, teaching, and assessing that many current educational arguments are traversing.

At base, I am advocating for a fundamental change in how we think about making sense of learners' developing cognition and understanding in history. In fact, I suggest that the typical testing approaches we have used for decades do precious little to make sense of student learning. As such, the data we commonly gather are relatively useless for improving that learning, or for adjusting teaching practices or curricula to facilitate it. I am hoping that my treatment of these issues on the pages that follow will go some distance toward addressing the good questions I have been hearing from those who have the most to gain from what I believe I am offering.

Bruce VanSledright
December 2012

1

THE NEED FOR NEW ASSESSMENTS IN HISTORY EDUCATION

In a book dealing with assessment in history education, it might make sense to begin with a short history test. So test your mettle with the one that follows. Grab a writing tool and read the directions, then assess yourself on these 12 straightforward questions. At the end of the test, you will find an answer key. That will allow you to check how well you fared. Now don't cheat by looking at the answers beforehand.

U.S. HISTORY TEST[1]

Directions: Read Each Question Carefully. Then Circle the Correct Answer.

1. An important part of President Woodrow Wilson's Fourteen Points was that

    A   A League of Nations was to be created.
    B   Germany had to surrender all its colonies.
    C   Reparation for war damages had to be paid to the Allies.
    D   The German Navy and Air Force had to give up the fight.

2.   Which of the following best describes an impact of European settlement during the colonial period on American Indians (First Americans)?

   A   Many American Indians died from European diseases.
   B   Many American Indian tribes used European military tactics to retain their lands.
   C   Many American Indians were educated in reservation schools.
   D   European settlers were unable to convert American Indians to Christianity.

3.   Immigrants in the late 19th century would most likely have been employed in which type of job?

   A   Manager
   B   Specialized craft worker
   C   Unskilled factory worker
   D   Salesperson

4.   After the Stock Market Crash in October 1929, there was

   A   A decrease in demand for consumer goods
   B   An increase in loans for buildings and factories
   C   A decrease in business failures
   D   An increase in industrial production

5.   What was the main reason for African American migration north between 1915 and 1925?

   A   Land prices fell in Midwestern states.
   B   Food prices were lower in urban areas.
   C   Immigrant communities were leaving Northern cities.
   D   Job opportunities increased in factories.

6.   Henry Ford's development of the assembly line led most directly to the growth of:

   A   City slums
   B   Child labor
   C   Industrial production
   D   Pollution problems

7. The United States' involvement in the Korean War was an example of the postwar policy of

   A Appeasement
   B Neutrality
   C Isolationism
   D Containment

8. Which of these immigrant groups came to America late in the 19th century and helped build the railroads?

   A Germans
   B Chinese
   C Polish
   D Haitians

9. The economy of the Southern colonies was based primarily on which of the following?

   A Agriculture
   B Fishing
   C Manufacturing
   D Mining

10. Which type of economic system is based on private ownership of property and the profit motive?

   A Traditional
   B Command
   C Subsistence
   D Capitalism

11. Money paid to the federal government by individuals comes mostly from taxes on

   A Their homes
   B Their income
   C Their gasoline purchases
   D Their food purchases

12. Which was a common characteristic of Nazi Germany, fascist Italy, and the Soviet Union?

    A They had similar economic policies.
    B They had the same religious beliefs.
    C They were ruled by dictatorships.
    D They had fought on the same side in World War I.

Answer key:	1. A	4. A	7. D	10. D
	2. A	5. D	8. B	11. B
	3. C	6. C	9. A	12. C

Putting how you scored aside for the moment, I would like to begin by making a series of observations about this "U.S. History Test" and particularly the items within it. First, this cluster of questions is drawn from the state of Virginia's Standards of Learning (SOL) year-end, high-stakes U.S. History test given to secondary students. These particular items come from those that the state has released. Second, as I am certain you noticed, the items sample across a temporal range extending from early British exploration and colonialism in North America through World War II. A few items also attempt to sample ideas about how capitalism is defined and where the federal government obtains the largest share of its revenue. In these senses, the range of items is designed to test students (and now you, if you took the test) not only for what they remember about historical events in America's past, but also about at least two concepts directly.

Third, I want to observe how familiar this test must seem. It is structured using the typical, traditional multiple-choice format, with three "wrong" options and only one "correct" one. Anyone currently living and who has been to school in the United States has undoubtedly taken a test at some point that looks something like this one, and likely more than once. They are simply ubiquitous. And fourth, I want to stress how scores on such tests, in Virginia and many other states as well, are used to make eventual decisions about whether students will receive a high school diploma, or instead will stand in line to receive some sort of remediation, including being held back.

Now I want to look more closely at what exactly such tests sample by way of historical knowledge, understanding, and thinking capability. The latter of these three represents the quality of being able to actually do something with the former two.

Because the ostensibly correct answer is supplied among the four options, this is more a test of a student's ability to identify or recognize that correct option. It is not much of a test of recall in the way someone might ask you at a social event who the 16th president of the United States was. If, therefore, a history student learns to become an astute test-taker, she can study the question prompt and attempt to ferret out the correct answer via textual context clues among the options. In this way the test is as much a measure of reading comprehension as it is a test of historical knowledge—and perhaps more so. However, if we put this concern on the sidebar for the moment, we can ask about what sorts of historical knowledge this 12-item test does sample.

Research over the past several decades on the nature of what it means to learn history is useful here.[2] Although not all history education researchers employ the following typology in exactly the same way, it does serve as a constructive guide for my purposes here. Knowledge in the domain of history can be roughly divided into two types: substantive (what, where, when, etc.) and strategic (how to get to the what, where, when, etc.). The division is only illustrative, however, because in learning history, each type of knowledge depends on the other and the boundaries separating them are decidedly porous. My brief treatment of these types of knowledge must suffice here, but I will return to them in more detail in the next chapter.

Substantive knowledge in history can be construed in two ways, again primarily for clarity and illustrative purposes. The first type is knowledge of who, what, where, when, how, and why questions (some call this first-order knowledge).[3] It also involves understanding definitions of such terms as revolution, democracy, and dictatorship that can serve as shorthand for larger clusters of ideas. This type of knowledge enables what we might call small- and big-picture narrativized or story-like understandings of the past, such as what the causes and consequences were for the Civil War or the Industrial Revolution.[4] The second type hinges on working with conceptual ideas that historical investigators impose on an unruly, complex past to bring some (artificial?) coherence to it in ways that enable deeper understanding. These include ideas such as progress/decline, change/continuity, historical significance, evidence for claims, and moral judgment. They are sometimes called second-order concepts. They have procedural components and so, in use, they bridge strategic and substantive knowledge. Therefore, some refer to them as substantive procedural concepts.[5]

Strategic knowledge involves possessing and deploying domain-specific strategies (i.e., thinking historically, the how to) for posing and answering rich historical questions that result in deeper understandings of the past. In other words, this means *doing* history, engaging in those cognitive efforts—*searching out* evidence, *assessing* the sources for what they may offer, *making sense* of the perspectives of the sources' authors, *judging* an author's reliability in making reputable claims—in service of answering historical questions of interest. Notice the active nature of doing here, represented in the italicized words. This thinking process also involves, as I noted, working with and applying second-order concepts to help manage and discipline that process. The result is first-order understanding—that is, knowing who, what, where, when, how, and why. Historical thinking, therefore, becomes the *sine qua non* of historical knowledge development and understanding.[6]

If we can return again to the "U.S. History Test" you just took, we can begin to see how much of this range of different types of knowledge it samples. If you look closely again at each item you will see that, at best, only a third of the types of knowledge I just described are tested. In fact, the 12 items sample exclusively first-order understandings: Wilson's "Fourteen Points," encounter impacts, 19th-century immigrant job types, consequences of the 1929 stock market crash, and so on. There are no items that test explicitly for knowledge of second-order concepts such as progress/decline, historical significance, or what constitutes historical evidence. Nor are there are items that test the capacity to think historically, such as how to arbitrate between two or three sources that offer conflicting testimony about what occurred at some seminal historical incident.

Based on this analysis and its subsequent observations, we might conclude that the test would produce an impoverished gauge of student understanding in history, at least the way the research work to which I alluded has defined it. Test- and policymakers in Virginia either have not read this research and consequently are unaware of the range of types of knowledge necessary to develop deeper historical understandings, believe that first-order knowledge is all that's worth testing, are convinced that it might be cost prohibitive to sample more than first-order ideas, or all or some combination of these. Regardless, as a measure of students' historical knowledge, the test appears oddly constrained and therefore tough to defend as a means by which to make high-stakes decisions about students' futures, particularly if we accept the research-based premise that historical thinking (aided by a working understanding of second-order concepts) is the *sine qua non* of historical understanding.

Given that premise, if you do not gauge the capacity to think historically, then it is possible to interpret test results that indicate passing scores as little more than the work of students who are good test-takers with powerful text comprehension skills rather than those who know their history. It's a bit like thinking it sufficient that a 16-year-old need only pass a written test to be licensed to drive a car, missing the point that the actual road test might matter more if skillful driving capability and reasonable road understanding are the goals.

★ ★ ★ ★ ★

Why is any of this worth noting? There are a number of reasons, including the importance of assessing historical thinking in addition to historical knowledge recall that I just described. But I would like to lay out several more that I believe bear closer scrutiny.

The "U.S. History Test" that you took earlier is a wildly popular approach to testing in history. Items like those in that test appear in many state history tests, from the New York Regents Exams to the Texas TAKS. I single out Virginia for no other reason than because its history testing practices are representative of my point and the ease of access to released items allow me to create an illustrative and representative example. Such items and practices also figure into the National Assessment of Educational Progress (NAEP) U.S. History tests, which pundits often call the testing "gold standard." Advanced Placement history tests have customarily employed similar practices and items. And history teachers have been drawn to these approaches for decades. In short, a whole high-stakes accountability regime is currently based upon this rather weak testing practice.

My point is that if we can identify Virginia SOL U.S. History tests as deeply limited in their approach to the assessment of historical thinking and understanding, then the same is true in many places across the United States, from large-sample national and statewide tests to individual classroom practices. Therefore, it would be fair to say that how we typically test in history misses the mark rather profoundly. Again, this is especially true if we accept the claim that historical thinking is the *sine qua non* of historical understanding.[7]

Testing as simple recall/recognition of a variety of historical terms, names, dates, and events, as I noted, fails to assess the full range of crucial forms of knowledge that enable historical understanding in the first place. Part of what may drive this impoverished approach to testing in history is the propensity among psychometricians and test developers to sacrifice construct validity to achieve adequate test reliability coefficients. In other words, if you elected to sample historical thinking (i.e., doing history), you would need tasks that allowed students to demonstrate their capabilities to think their way through historical problems, such as how to interpret what caused the Boston Massacre in 1770.

The evidence a student would need to accomplish this interpretive feat is complex and in conflict, pushing her to study that evidence and write out an explanation that drew from it. Here's the real rub: Scoring this sort of task quickly transcends applications of item-response theory and simple correct/incorrect judgments. Put simply, more complex tasks that assess doing history (e.g., the document-based question) rapidly become more expensive to score and more tricky from a reliability standpoint. For many testmakers and state departments of education, these issues are unappealing. However, as we have seen, there are other opportunity costs that are incurred, particularly the loss of capacity to measure crucial thinking capabilities. This begs the question: Are our common, typical approaches to testing sufficient to establish that someone who has achieved a passing score is a person who understands history?

A second reason worth observing effectively begs another question that underpins the one I just raised. Even if we assume—albeit perhaps spuriously—that a passing score represents someone who understands history, how many achieve passing scores? We have no hard evidence that most attain such a grade. If we appeal to the NAEP "gold standard" test results in U.S. history, for example, we find that approximately every five years or so, very few students tested attain proficiency. Proficiency here can be thought of as a close cousin to understanding, at least of first-order ideas. The most recent NAEP U.S. History test was given to a cross section of the nation's fourth, eighth, and twelfth graders in 2009–2010. The current report's executive summary states, "The percentage of students performing at or above the Proficient level in 2010 was 20 percent at grade 4, 17 percent at grade 8, and 12 percent at grade 12."[8]

Going backward through previous NAEP U.S. History test score results simply confirms at least two decades of similar outcomes. And before NAEP U.S. History testing began in the 1980s, there were other national tests given to cross sections of students in the country that produced equally dismal results.[9] In the United States, the common obsession of using U.S. history courses to teach the narrative of national development, asking students to commit this narrative to memory, and testing their recall of the details of this narrative shows that such an approach consistently does precious little to produce understanding or proficiency. As such, there is little to recommend it. We need new teaching and testing approaches if historical understanding is the goal. The Virginia testing strategy and the many others like it, and the way they effectively compel history teachers to approach the subject pedagogically, simply will not do.

A third reason worth noting is the appearance of a history strand in the latest English/Language Arts (ELA) Common Core (CC) Standards. The ELA CC Standards have been embraced by more than

40 states (Virginia and Texas not among them) and the District of Columbia, therefore are likely to affect a majority of the nation's school-age children and adolescents. States have already begun the shift away from their previous state-specific standards documents and have put local education agencies (LEAs) on notice that they need to prepare teachers for their infusion, and apparently for subsequent shifts in high-stakes tests aligned with them.

With regard to the ELA history strand, what do these standards ask that students be able to do? A look at a small cluster of these standards demonstrates that, if the standard's indicators are to be achieved, students will need to show that they have the knowledge *to do history* as well as the capability to simply recall it or recognize its elements from within options. Here are three standards from the section dealing with eleventh and twelfth grade history:

> RH11–12.1.1. Cite specific textual, visual, or physical evidence to support analysis of primary and secondary sources, connecting insights gained from specific details to a [historical] understanding . . .
>
> RH11–12.3.3. Evaluate various explanations for actions or events and determine which explanation best accords with source evidence, acknowledging where sources leave matters uncertain.
>
> RH11–12.8.8. Evaluate an author's premises, claims, and evidence by corroborating or challenging them with other sources or accounts.[10]

A focus on the verbs in each example helps demonstrate what students will need to be able to do. In the first case, students will need to be able to "cite," "support" (analysis), and "connect" (insights). In the second case, they must be able to "evaluate," "determine," and "acknowledge." The third case requires "evaluation" again, along with "corroborating" and "challenging." These verbs represent thinking capabilities by any other name.

Examining the objects of these thinking capabilities provides a second window onto what students must be able to do. It gives some insight into the conceptual, second-order understandings they must hold in order to achieve these standards. In RH11–12.1.1, we see "evidence" and "sources." The term *sources* implies "accounts" from the past. These are multiple since the terms are pluralized and they are further qualified by a distinction between "primary" and "secondary" versions. In RH11–12.3.3, "evidence" reappears along with "explanations" and "uncertainty." In the third case, we see the concept of "evidence" and "sources/accounts" yet again, coupled with an "author" and "premises" and "claims."

Taken together, we can envision the sorts of practices and activities ELA CC authors believe history students need to have undertaken by the time they graduate. They clearly include both types of knowledge—second-order substantive and strategic (cognitive)—that are seldom assessed by current and typical testing approaches. The wide adoption of these standards purports to significantly affect teaching and learning, meaning that current testing practice will need to shift, and quite dramatically, if states wish to claim that their testing approaches align satisfactorily with the ELA CC. Recall/recognition of a handful of historical details, terms, and names is simply insufficient to claim historical understanding under the ELA CC umbrella. But what should the new assessments look like? If these three indicators are any guide, students will need to be doing extensive reading, thinking, and writing in history, and ostensibly on assessments also. In short, the ELA CC Standards would appear to require students to engage in *doing-history* performances on assessments without actually stipulating them. Yet very few students in the United States are currently asked to perform history on tests with stakes that affect their futures.[11] Aligning assessment practice to these new standards will necessitate new thinking and new exemplars.

A final window onto what will be asked of students requires a bit of telepathy. The Common Core Standards initiative took up English/language arts and mathematics. The social studies (including history) and science domains were left unattended. However, organizations such as the National Council for the Social Studies, with a variety of partners including the Council of Chief State School Officers (CCSSO), undertook to craft a state inquiry framework for history, geography, economics, and government. As I write this book, the framework has yet to be released. Word has it, though, that a least to a pivotal degree, they will incorporate a number of the elements of the historical thinking, reading, and writing strands of the ELA CC. Somewhere in the vicinity of 25 states have expressed interest in the inquiry framework for social studies. To the extent that the final document aligns with the ELA CC and states choose to adopt social studies framework, we have yet another reason to anticipate the need for a fairly profound shift in assessment design and practice in history education.

★ ★ ★ ★ ★

In 2001, after a thorough review of extant testing practices across the country, both high-stakes and low, the Committee on the Foundations of Assessment, led by James Pellegrino, Naomi Chudowsky, and Robert Glaser, issued their final report via the National Research Council. In the Executive Summary, the authors note:

> Every assessment, regardless of purpose, rests on three pillars: a [theoretical] model of how students represent knowledge and develop competence in the subject domain, tasks or situations that allow one to observe students' performance, and an interpretation method for drawing inferences from the performance evidence thus obtained.[12]

The report provides an overview of thinking about assessing what students know, reasoning from assessment evidence, theoretical models of domain learning and teaching, and contributions of measurement and statistical modeling to assessment design, in addition to detailing principles and practices (with many examples) for constructing valid and valuable assessments. The authors begin and conclude with a compelling call to use knowledge of assessment principles to reshape assessment practices, following the three pillars they initially describe—however, not many states and testmakers noticed after the passage of the *No Child Left Behind* legislation.

At its date of release, the report was one of most comprehensive accounts of assessment thinking available. It is now more than a decade

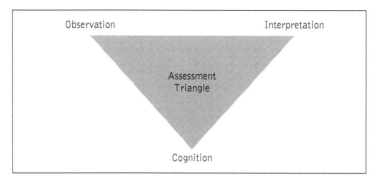

FIGURE 1.1. The Committee's Assessment Triangle.[13]

old. However, it is almost as if the committee could foresee the arrival of the ELA Common Core, for example. The report continues to hold sound advice for reworking assessments of student knowledge and thinking capabilities. Therefore, I draw heavily from it for thinking about and reshaping history assessment practices. In particular, I organize this book in large measure around the three assessment pillars: (a) a theoretical model of domain learning and competence, (b) tasks and situations that permit performative observations of targeted learning goals, and (c) an interpretation method for inferring from evidence such observations produce. The committee refers to the interaction among these three pillars as the assessment triangle.

Structure

In order to accomplish my plan in the chapters that follow, I begin in Chapter 2 with a small-t theoretical model of thinking in the history domain. I link this model to images of what constitutes competence in historical thinking and understanding. More than three decades of research in history education allow me to weave ideas about cognitive progressions from novice to competent variations into this consideration with categorizations of expertise employed as benchmarks. I draw on investigative types of teaching practices as touchstones for inviting and encouraging students to become competent historical thinkers who can understand both the past and history. To draw illustrative examples, some of these practices implicate the standards related to the ELA CC that I already described.

Chapter 3 begins with some classroom context in order to take up tasks and situations that portend suitability for gauging the types of historical thinking efforts that beget understanding. I sample a variety of strategies, designs, and approaches that I suspect will yield powerful evidence of students' capabilities. These range from decidedly untraditional multiple-choice items to complex document-based question designs. However, there will be examples readers will know about or have used themselves that are also instructive, but not ones I have considered or consider here. I try to be as concrete as I can with the examples I provide.

Chapter 4 deals with interpretation schemes. It builds on the examples in detailed in Chapter 3. Scoring systems, rubrics, evidence analyses, and the like are paired with those examples. Inferring evidence from tasks and situations is a complex matter, characterized by limits that derive from the nature of those tasks and situations. I try to be cautious here and suggest reasonable boundaries, such as indicating high- and low-inference interpretations when they are fitting. Again, I make every effort to provide concrete examples (scoring guides, rubrics, coding schemes) to illustrate the evidence-interpretation process. Some readers may disagree, thinking the inference liberties I take are unwarranted. I welcome such observations. I can be reached at <bvansled@uncc.edu>.

In the final chapter, I attempt to stitch together the ideas outlined in the previous chapters. I summarize and synthesize. The key theme of this final chapter is alignment: aligning a history curriculum and standards (opportunities to learn) with a theory of cognitive development in the history domain—one that begets investigative teaching approaches—with the shaping of assessment strategies and interpretation schemes. Doing so serves as a primer, one designed to identify a clustered and aligned approach to history education assessment, whose examples can yield valuable evidence of student learning progressions.

Assumptions and Clarifications

My principal goal here involves entering into and expanding on conversations about assessing historical thinking and understanding in ways that we have typically not done with much fervor in the past. Yes, we have experimented with variations on some of the ideas I suggest. But we have not systematically undertaken to build a coherent and theoretically aligned set of practices that provide us with more than numerical test scores, whose usefulness seems increasingly dubious.

A key assumption I make is that the most useful and constructive evidence of student learning (or the lack of it) in history is most valuable to teachers. To paraphrase David Cohen and Susan Moffitt, if we wish to improve teaching and learning, then we have to focus on teaching and learning. In the case of history education, that means turning attention to how history teachers can teach to improve upon how students learn.[14] To this end, the ideas I pursue and the concrete examples I provide are targeted at measuring student learning in ways that can give those teachers more or less immediate feedback on what's happening with their students. Some call this formative assessment. I prefer to think that all carefully aligned assessment is fundamentally formative (perhaps even performative), meaning that it generates evidence on how students' historical ideas are developing.[15]

If assessment practices work this way, they provide teachers with formative, diagnostic feedback on both student learning and teaching practice. In the case of the latter, formative, diagnostic feedback provided by formative, diagnostic assessments regarding student learning occasions the opportunity to adjust those practices to improve that learning. I am much less concerned here with what some call summative assessments, or end-of-year tests that function as forms of overall program evaluation. However, this is not to say that the ideas and examples I entertain in what follows would have not utility for these types of "summative assessment" efforts. In fact, they might be highly applicable. I simply allude to such applications in the final chapter without pursuing them at any length.

Because of my interest in teaching and learning history and the fundamental role formative, diagnostic assessment can play in it, I do not discuss here the technical matters associated with large-scale testing, say, on a state-wide or national basis. By this I mean that I skirt concerns about "item performance," "bi-serial correlations," "reliability coefficients," and the like. This is the realm of test psychometrics. This book is meant primarily to be a concise primer on classroom-based assessment with powerful formative and diagnostic components designed to improve historical thinking and the understandings that follow from it.

Part of the reason I tread only around the edges of test psychometrics involves my worry over what has often happened with large-scale testing practices once the concerns surrounding the interpretation of thousands of students' test results enter in. First, as I have implied reliability (whether test items are discriminating properly, as on a bell curve distribution) becomes almost an obsession, frequently to the exclusion of what I would term concerns over construct validity (assessing the pivotal processes and ideas that constitute understanding). The test you took at the beginning of this chapter and the items that test includes serve as a case in point.

In my estimation, the opening 12-item test example, while it may be wonderfully reliable in that it produces consistent results over widely variable populations, has astonishingly low construct validity. It maps only onto an exceptionally small segment of the range of knowledge in and of history, the constructs that make history history, and the conceptual and cognitive apparatus that enables someone to understand history. Therefore, I would argue that it comes very close to being construct *invalid*. If it is a domain-invalid test because it hews to a deeply impoverished cognitive and sociocultural model of learning, it possesses in turn little if any formative, diagnostic power for the very people who need construct-valid evidence of learning the most—history teachers (and also students as they learn to become self-assessors). I am assuming that more often than not, when reliability concerns trump construct validity, as they appear to do in the test example I provided, there is little further to be said other than what I have already noted.

For these reasons, I prefer to make the case for formative assessments with stronger construct validity and leave the scaling-up, overall program-evaluation worries to others. However, I still hope they can learn from the examples I provide and gamble on putting such assessment practices in play while solving the psychometric problems that can arise in doing so.

Learning history is a thorny undertaking largely because the domain is a complicated one with a number of counterintuitive characteristics.

Everyday ideas about the past, much like everyday ideas about the solar system (e.g., the child's visual observation that the sun orbits the Earth), have limited utility for cultivating deeper understanding. To achieve a degree of construct validity, and obtain evidence of students' developing understandings of those constructs, demands complex assessment strategies. As test developers well know, when complexity increases, so does cost. I would be remiss in failing to call attention to that fact here. At the same time, if we are to steer much needed attention toward improving teaching and learning in and of history, we are simply going to need more complex, construct-valid assessments that sample a much wider span of historical understandings.

Costs, both in human resource terms (e.g., the intellectual energy consumed to produce such assessments) and in real monetary commitments, certainly accompany the sorts of assessment approaches I propose. Yet I think it's time to invest more in teachers and students with evaluation strategies that actually improve on the work they do. Testing on the cheap, as a form of regulation, has done little to significantly improve schools because cheap tests produce cheap results.[16] To be blunt, I am making the assumption that it is long since past time for investing in more elaborate, useful assessment strategies that promise (per)formative, diagnostic power for teachers and learners. In any case, for those states adopting the ELA Common Core Standards, more costly performative assessments will become a necessity if states seek adequate alignments between the standards and evidence of their achievement.

New Assessment Research and Development

Anticipating the necessity of different types of assessment strategies, groups and organizations already have waded in. Two testing organizations' efforts are notable. At Educational Testing Service (ETS), assessment developers launched CBAL (Cognitively-Based Assessment *of, for*, and *as* Learning) several years ago.[17] CBAL researchers have begun building performance-based assessments that intentionally or otherwise align with a number of the standards in the ELA Common Core.

A consortium of states, armed with a grant from the federal government, formed SBAC, or Smarter Balanced Assessment Consortium.

SBAC has begun extensive work on building assessments that align directly with the common core in ELA and Mathematics.[18] SBAC somewhat lags behind ETS's CBAL in item development largely because it began work later, has a broader more challenging task, and represents a large consortium with a wide range of stakeholders who seek input.

What is worth observing here is that both organizations' item-development work is geared more directly to the ELA Common Core—that is, more toward reading comprehension, literacy development, and progression markers of reading and writing capability. In my judgment, I find that, even though there are some items that reference the history portion of the ELA Common Core, the items do not assess the forms of historical knowledge and understanding I have alluded to in this chapter and will detail in the next. This is not a criticism per se. Item development in these two organizations reflects a time-worn (over?) emphasis on early reading and literacy frequently untethered to specific forms of knowledge in school subject domains such as history.[19] In short, a close reading of the ELA Common Core reveals that it is silent on *what* historical knowledge and understandings students should obtain. Although this might be understandable given the ELA's literacy focus, some of the standards as written (and because of their silence regarding necessary knowledge) can be construed as unintentionally undermining historical thinking and understanding.[20]

For example, within the ELA Common Core, a distinction is made between literary texts and information texts. History texts seem to be linked to the latter in terms of the ways in which some early test-item developments appear aligned theoretically. This is rather typical. History is frequently cast as a type of neutral information conveyor belt. Yet history shares much more in common with literature, and therefore its texts can be better thought of as literary traces rather than informational texts. This distinction is far from trivial when it comes to designing assessment items because how knowledge and understanding are conceived as assessment targets profoundly shapes how assessment items are written, or at least they should be written. Assessing history as mere "information" masks its deep interpretive and perspectival character and obscures texts as traces or *residua* from the past that need careful "literary"-like interpretation. Thinking of and testing history as "information" can significantly warp how it is ultimately perceived and block how it is understood.

Therefore, with respect to these two organizations' efforts, what I suggest in the following pages is a relatively unique treatment of assessment issues and development within a specific knowledge domain. Put a different way, my treatment inverts the relationship between literacy and a subject matter, in this case history. Instead of foregrounding general literacy practices as targets to be assessed with the particular subject matter serving as little more than a vehicle for the content of an item (as my reading suggests both CBAL and SBAC have done to date), I am proposing to make historical knowledge and understanding the primary targets, with literacy practices serving as vehicles that enable that knowledge and understanding. Through this inversion, I am hoping to address an open niche created by (a) an emphasis on literacy for its own sake understandably favored in ELA-type standards and (b) an anticipated release of a social studies state inquiry framework, including the history domain, that authors indicate will be in part aligned to the ELA Common Core. The social studies framework may help specify part of the missing *what* of historical understanding while also cohering to some degree with the *how* (historical thinking) alluded to in the ELA Common Core.

A third organization's developments that are worth noting emerge from the Centre for Historical Consciousness at the University of British Columbia. In 2006, the group released "Benchmarks for Historical Thinking."[21] Recently, they have begun testing assessment items constructed to measure outcomes tied to those benchmarks. The benchmarks feed a cognitive model for learning history that bears some similarity to the model I discuss in Chapter 2. Assessment item development to date and item-validation work has concentrated on multiple-choice questions and types of document-based questions rooted in three second-order historical concepts: evidence, perspective taking, and the ethical dimension (moral judgment).[22] Interested readers will notice some overlap between the assessment strategies and items emerging from the Canadian group's work and what I am proposing largely because of commonalities attributable to shared features of the cognitive learning model, even though the Canadian work does not stipulate the cognitive model very clearly.

Finally, my research and development work over the last 10 years with the Teaching American History Program Evaluation Team at the University of Maryland, College Park, has significantly influenced the assessment examples and interpretation practices that frame Chapters 3 and 4.[23] In our work as program evaluators of six large Teaching American History grants, we sought to develop novel assessment strategies. Although this work involved assessing changes in history teachers' knowledge, understanding, and historical thinking capabilities as they moved through the grants' intervention processes, much of the assessment theorizing and development we undertook are applicable to students in modified form. Like those at the Centre for Historical Consciousness, we designed, constructed, pilot-tested, and validated our methods based on a sociocultural cognitive model of learning in the history domain. Many of the items we employed in our evaluation figure deeply into the examples I provide.

Summary

By all accounts, we need new assessments if we wish to make sense of how students learn history. These assessments would do well if they served history teachers and students first. Because teachers are at the very forefront of improving students' thinking capabilities and understandings, they would benefit from diagnostic assessment approaches and strategies that provide more or less immediate feedback on how their students' historical ideas are progressing from novice status to more competent and proficient. This in turn requires a robust and detailed sociocultural cognitive model of learning in the domain. It also requires construct-valid assessment tasks and situations and equally robust methods of drawing interpretations from the data they generate. In keeping with the structure I proposed, I sequentially lay out a learning domain model, describe a variety of assessment tasks and situations mapped to that model, and then identify a series of sturdy evidence-interpretation strategies that yield defensible methods of making sense of what students do with, think about, and understand in history.

Notes

1 This "U.S. History Test" is a very slightly modified collection (e.g., reduced word count, minor grammar adjustments) of questions and an answer key drawn from items the state of Virginia released to the public in 2007 from its Standards of Learning high-stakes, end-of-year history tests. Such items are searchable at http://www.doe.virginia.gov/testing/sol/released_tests/index.shtml.

2 See detailed reviews of this work by Keith Barton, "Research on Students' Ideas About History," in Linda Levstik and Cynthia Tyson (Eds.), *Handbook of Research in Social Studies Education* (New York: Routledge, 2008), pp. 239–258; Peter Lee, "Putting Principles Into Practice: Understanding History," in Susan Donovan and John Bransford (Eds.), *How Students Learn: History in the Classroom* (Washington, DC: National Academies Press, 2005), pp. 31–78; Bruce VanSledright and Margarita Limon, "Learning and Teaching in Social Studies: Cognitive Research on History and Geography," in Patricia Alexander and Phillip Winne (Eds.), *The Handbook of Educational Psychology, 2nd Ed.* (Mahwah, NJ: Lawrence Erlbaum Associates, 2006), pp. 545–570; James Voss, "Issues in the Learning of History," *Issues in Education: Contributions From Educational Psychology, 4* (1998), pp. 183–209; and Sam Wineburg, *Historical Thinking and Other Unnatural Acts: Charting the Future of Teaching the Past* (Philadelphia: Temple University Press, 2001), Chapter 2.

3 See Peter Lee, "Putting Principles Into Practice."

4 See, for example, Jonathan Howson and Denis Shemilt, "Frameworks of Knowledge: Dilemmas and Debates," in Ian Davies (Ed.), *Debates in History Teaching* (London: Routledge, 2011), pp. 73–83.

5 See Lee, "Putting Principles."

6 One does not simply know history or the past. One needs to do the complex and active work of thinking about and through the past in order to understand it. Memorizing historical details may count as a form of thinking, but it is a very weak species of cognition and is far from sufficient for obtaining understanding.

7 I wish to point out that this is no idle claim. Studies of experts engaged in problem-solving tasks, ones who lacked specific knowledge of the subject in question (e.g., Abraham Lincoln) and others who possessed it, have shown that the former were able to think their way to an understanding of the problem posed by the question precisely because they were able to draw on their disciplinary cognitive capabilities in the task settings. For one such study in history, see Sam Wineburg, "Reading Abraham

Lincoln: An Expert-Expert Study in the Interpretation of Historical Texts," *Cognitive Science, 22* (1998), pp. 319–346.

8 See the summary and links to full test results online at http://nces.ed.gov/pubsearch/pubsinfo.asp?pubid=2011468.

9 See Sam Wineburg, *Historical Thinking*, Chapter 2.

10 These ELA CC Standards and their history strands are available online at http://www.corestandards.org/the-standards/english-language-arts-standards.

11 See, for example, S.G. Grant (Ed.), *Measuring History [Achievement]: Cases of State-Level Testing Across the United States* (Greenwich, CT: Information Age Publishing, 2006).

12 James Pellegrino, Naomi Chudowsky, and Robert Glaser (Eds.), *Knowing What Students Know: The Science and Design of Educational Assessment* (Washington, DC: National Academies Press, 2001), p. 2.

13 Pellegrino, Chudowsky, and Glaser, p. 44.

14 See David K. Cohen and Susan L. Moffitt, *The Ordeal of Equality: Did Federal Regulation Fix the Schools?* (Cambridge, MA: Harvard University Press, 2009).

15 For more on the distinction, or the lack of one, between formative and summative assessments, see Michael Scriven, *Evaluation Thesaurus, 4th Ed.* (Newbury Park, CA: Sage, 1991).

16 See, for example, Cohen and Moffitt, *The Ordeal*; Linda Darling-Hammond, "The Implications of Testing Policy for Quality and Equality," in *Phi Delta Kappan, 73* (1991), pp. 218–224; and Georgia Earnest Garcia and P. David Pearson, "Assessment and Diversity," in Linda Darling-Hammond (Ed.), *Review of Educational Research, 20* (1994), pp. 337–391.

17 For more on these developments at ETS, see http://www.ets.org/research/topics/cbal/initiative.

18 For details, see http://www.k12.wa.us/smarter/.

19 To make this point clear, Timothy and Cynthia Shanahan note that the U.S. federal government had invested, through 2008, $5 billion into "Reading First," an early literacy program, while contributing only $30 million to "Striving Readers," an adolescent, subjects-based reading program. See Timothy Shanahan and Cynthia Shanahan, "Teaching Disciplinary Literacy to Adolescents: Rethinking Content-Area Literacy," *Harvard Educational Review, 78* (Spring 2008), pp. 40–59.

20 For a pointed discussion of the variety of ways in which this occurs in common reading programs, see Bruce VanSledright, "Learning With History Texts: Protocols for Reading and Practical Strategies," in Tamara Jetton and Cynthia Shanahan (Eds.), *Adolescent Literacy Within Disciplines: General Principles and Practical Strategies* (New York: Guilford), pp. 199–226.

21 This document can be viewed at the center's website. See http://histori calthinking.ca/documents/benchmarks-historical-thinking-framework-assessment-canada.

22 See, for example, Kadriye Ercikan, Peter Seixas, Juliette Lyons-Thomas, and Lindsay Gibson, "Designing and Validating an Assessment of Historical Thinking Using Evidence-Centered Assessment Design," a paper presented at the American Educational Research Association annual meeting (Vancouver, BC, April 2012).

23 For explanations of portions of this work and reflections on the developmental process, see Liliana Maggioni, Bruce VanSledright, and Patricia Alexander, "Walking on the Borders: A Measure of Epistemic Cognition in History," *Journal of Experimental Education*, 77 (2009), pp. 187–213; Liliana Maggioni, Patricia Alexander, and Bruce VanSledright, "At the Crossroads: The Development of Epistemological Beliefs and Historical Thinking." *European Journal of School Psychology, 2* (2004), pp. 169–197; Bruce VanSledright, "The Challenge of Assessing American History Knowledge Development Among Teachers," *National History Education Clearinghouse* (2008), available online at http://teachinghistory.org/tah-grants/lessons-learned/19432; and Bruce VanSledright, Kevin Meuwissen, and Timothy Kelly, "Oh, the Trouble We've Seen: Researching Historical Thinking and Understanding," in Keith Barton (Ed.), *Research Methods in Social Studies Education: Contemporary Issues and Perspectives* (Greenwich, CT: Information Age Publishing, 2006), pp. 207–233.

For the idea of designing and using weighted multiple-choice items in history, I am indebted to conversations I have had with Patricia Alexander especially. Liliana Maggioni, who has read just about everything ever written about epistemic beliefs in history (and other subjects as well), has helped to push my thinking about ways to assess those beliefs. Timothy Kelly and Kevin Meuwissen made it a point to argue with me regularly about my positions on assessing understanding. Those discussions also pushed my thinking in ways I was unclear about at the time. The Teaching American History (TAH) grant program may have produced mixed results in its mission of growing the knowledge of history teachers. For us TAH program evaluators, however, it was a powerful seedbed for exploring new ways of developing assessments that could provide rich evidence of what it means to come to understand the past. Many of those ideas have found their way onto the following pages.

2

A SOCIOCULTURAL COGNITIVE MODEL FOR LEARNING HISTORY

In *Knowing What Students Know: The Science and Design of Educational Assessment*, James Pellegrino, Naomi Chudowsky, and Robert Glaser observe, "A model of cognition and learning should serve as the cornerstone of the assessment design process."[1] Later, they add, "...assessment will be most effective if the designer (in many cases the teacher) *starts* with an explicit and clearly conceptualized cognitive model of learning."[2] The model, they argue, needs to be rooted in a robust understanding of how students learn and develop competence in a particular domain. That understanding should be derived from the latest cognitive and educational research. They point out that without such a model, assessment designs and the evidence they generate will be impoverished and as a result produce questionable and/or spurious interpretations of what students know and can do with what they know. We saw a *prima facie* example of that in the early section of the last chapter.

I want to follow the advice these authors provide by beginning with one such model in history education. Contrary to popular opinion, one does not simply come to "know history" because he or she has read and memorized the details of history books and teachers' lectures. Knowing history does not emerge solely from some accumulative process, as if to know and understand depends upon a steady accretion of historical tidbits and facts woven together by someone's narrative. This may help some, but it is far from sufficient. Historical understanding, I will say again, follows from a complex process of thinking historically. It is a practice that forms in a community of investigators, investigators who pose questions, think hard about what remains from the past that may (or may not always) help answer those questions, and wrestle with and debate what they come up with. Perspective is pivotal and it precipitates the debates. Perspective depends on a raft of sociocultural and temporal anchors that vary with identity, beliefs, and values. Therefore, historical understanding is variable, and this is what can make it far from simple, but on the other hand, also so fascinating.

One acquires this sort of historical thinking or cognition by participating in a community of practice that is designed to gradually sharpen cognitive capability.[3] A more knowledgeable other (a history teacher), armed with a robust theory of thinking and learning in the domain, looks for cognitive progression markers. She anticipates where difficulties will arise and attempts to assist learners in adjusting for them. Key impediments in learning how to think historically in ways that will produce understanding frequently hinge on those sociocultural and temporal anchors that learners bring with them to the learning community.

Sociocultural Anchors

Many of these anchors were developed outside this history learning community, at home, in the marketplace, on the Internet, and through the consumption of mass-culture events via television or YouTube for example. They become ingrained because they appear to hold powerful intuitive appeal. The role of history teachers, then, is to identify how these anchors create learning impasses and help learners get over on them. This is difficult, for many of these anchors, and the ideas that flow from them, are so taken for granted and buried from view that learners have difficulty both in picking them out in the first place and then in changing how they think, believe, and value in the second place. Historical thinking requires the development of several significant counterintuitive modes of thought, ones that resist intuitive but unproductive anchoring. Those counterintuitive modes lead to understanding. This is where a robust, socioculturally rooted cognitive model or theory of thinking in history becomes most valuable.

I want to begin by illustrating several of these intuitively held anchors that have their origins in the everyday growth of epistemic beliefs. Then I will move to discussing more productive types of thinking efforts that learners need to undertake in the community of practice we call history, those emerging from the educational research that I endnoted in Chapter 1. With some luck, this will produce a model of cognition that can lead to more effective assessments. In turn, those assessments can provide useful, diagnostic data for teachers that allow them to reorient their practices. Those reorientations can enhance the thinking and understanding of students in ways common assessment practices of the past have not made possible.

Counterproductive Epistemic Beliefs

Arguably, the most significant impediments to historical understanding are assumptions we are prone to make about what history is, where it comes from, and how its knowledge claims are justified. People consistently confuse the past with history, often conflating the two. Ask any fifth grader what history is and he will likely remark that it is the past. Many adults are known to make the same remark. History is what happened in the past, as if the two were isomorphic. However, formulating a distinction between the two could not be more important.

The past, of course, is all those events and incidents that have gone on in the world of human experience before this moment. The scope of the past is mindbending. It is complex, unwieldy, and resists full comprehension. The key point here is realizing that our access to the past is mediated by *residue* and *relics* (hereafter simply residue): the sorts of texts, paintings, and pottery shards that carry over to us in the present day. These remains are all the access we have. We cannot go back and recreate the past to "see what really happened." As historian Joan Wallach Scott observes, we wish to tell the truth about the past as we try to understand it. But this act is denied because the residue and relics never provide us a complete story, and authentic recreation and time travel are impossible.[4] So, despite our very best efforts, we can still get it wrong or become misguided even if only unintentionally.

History emerges as distinct from the past in that it is the name we give to our efforts to interpret the past, to tell stories about what it means. It cannot be isomorphic with the past. It is particularistic, selective, laced with perspective. History—try as it might to get it right, to tell the singular truth—is not univocal. The word *history* more aptly describes a practice of interpreting the past. Its result is histories—plural. Histories multiply every day as historical investigators interpret and reinterpret the past. New sociocultural anchors among investigators and newly discovered residue produce new histories over the top of older ones. It's an ongoing practice, old enough to foster a busy subdiscipline called historiography in which investigators attempt to describe the ever-changing landscape of emerging historical interpretations.

The problem with equating the history with the past is at least twofold. First, if a student makes that assumption, he misses the whole of the complex interpretive process that must be undertaken in order to make sense of the past. That interpretive process, or historical thinking by another name, is how understanding is achieved if it is done well and thoroughly. And second, the result is that our student assumes, for instance, that a history text's words map directly onto the past. This creates an illusion that history falls out of the sky readymade.

This may seem comforting at first, but the illusion is unmasked as soon as multiple histories or multiple interpretations of the past that conflict and/or contradict each other come into view. And multiple versions are everywhere, from contradictory claims about what events from the past mean on the Internet to even a cursory examination of what two different school textbooks—a British one and one from the United States—say happened during the Boston "Massacre." These inevitable encounters with contradiction, sans skilled interpretive practices, produce cognitive impasses that block historical understanding.

One solution to this problem of contradiction that novices are quick to employ arises from a form of dichotomous thinking learned early in life away from school. A child goes to play outdoors and wanders some distance from home. Caught up in the pleasures of exploring new landscapes or playing with friends, she comes home past the time father has commanded as the return hour. The child learns quickly, with introductions of parental vocabulary, that she can either tell the truth (e.g., I was having great fun with my friends and simply ignored your command) or make up a lie that will sound palatable enough to avoid father's wrath. So, she begins to conclude, accountings can either lie or tell the truth. To fend off contradictions and conflicts among historical accounts, this same logic frequently is applied. One account is lying while the other is telling the truth.

With novices, however, the capacity to think through the differences, and use criteria to separate them, is frequently absent. Therefore, determining the truth from the lie in history is difficult if not impossible. Unproductive inventive thinking often comes into play at this point.[5] Or, if there is a group involved, someone may suggest that the problem can be resolved through voting on which is the truthful account. Neither "solution" fixes the problem. The adequate judging of claims to knowledge is thus compromised. Historical understanding ultimately suffers.

Beliefs About Texts and Reading

Historical accounts commonly appear in some textual form (even pictures and movies are forms of text that must be read and interpreted). Novice thinkers also hold common but unproductive beliefs about texts and where they come from. First, they rarely observe that texts have authors unless they are specifically prompted to pay attention to those authors. Second, even when prompted, novices think that if an author was smart enough to write a book, for example, he or she must be believable. Third, they take for granted that the words in a text correspond directly to what they describe, what Roland Barthes once called the "referential illusion."[6] Under the referential illusion, claims to knowledge need no justification; they are pre-justified by virtue of how their wording corresponds directly to reality.

Because novices fail to recognize the perspectival, interpretive presence of an author, they also miss the fact that historical authors can use the same words and phrases to mean different things. Their meaning-making and understanding, therefore, become deeply confused despite applications of a variety of reading and thinking practices with powerful intuitive appeal, some of which are taught at home and in the early years at school. One example would be the ubiquitous request to "find a paragraph's main, singular idea." The request implies that texts are straightforward and mean just what they say. To fuss about it—to say it might have more than one main idea, for example—would be silly.

Early practices in learning to read in school, akin to the one I just mentioned parenthetically, often create what Robert Scholes calls textual fundamentalists.[7] These are readers who are taught to succumb to the referential illusion that words in a text map directly onto a reality that they describe. Even the language of the ELA Common Core Standards designed to guide 21st-century reading and writing development appears to succumb to this illusion. As I remarked in the last chapter, the ELA Common Core makes a running distinction between "literary" texts and "informational" texts. Histories seem to fall in with the latter. Literary texts need interpretation because they are fictional. Informational texts, because they appear to convey "information" directly without fictional intent, apparently do not. In historical study, this distinction could not be less helpful.

In history, in some very real way all texts must be interpreted. Because author perspective is so crucial to understanding and because authors' sociocultural positioning varies, authors can describe the very same historical event in markedly different ways. In addition, some authors have been known to self-contradict *within* the same history text. This does not mean necessarily that one author is lying and one is telling the truth, or that all histories are fictions, although as Hayden White has noted, many of them contain fictions.[8] As such, history students, at some difficulty, must be disabused of the idea that history texts (original or synthetic, it doesn't matter) fall in the category of informational texts. They would be more aptly taught early on that all history texts are literary devices (literary texts?) of one sort or another—that they require interpretation, and need to be understood that way. The ELA Common Core document would offer better advice if it dropped the literary/informational text distinction when it comes to learning in history. As we can see, it cultivates more trouble here than it resolves.

Novices approach histories with ingrained epistemic beliefs—about how the world and texts in the world work—that can inhibit and block deeper historical understandings. These beliefs must be identified and changed through deliberate educational efforts if these novices are to make progress in making sense of the past. Counterproductive epistemic beliefs, because they are so often taken for granted, will not simply disappear as students learn more historical facts and details. Novices need to be immersed in a process that teaches them how to think historically in order for them to proceed to more profound understandings of the past. Reading histories, albeit important, is but only one small part of the process, as the aforementioned reviews of research studies have taught us.

Just as a novice's early, intuitive epistemic beliefs encourage textual fundamentalism and a form of naïve realism or objectivism about history (e.g., the past and history are one and the same), a growing, educated awareness of the influence of sociocultural positioning can initially encourage an equally counterproductive form of naïve relativism or subjectivism about understanding the past (e. g., the past is whatever I interpret it to be). One set of unproductive beliefs often gets traded in for another.

There are powerful tensions here that affect how we think about and understand the past. On the one hand, epistemic anchors that flow from our beliefs about how the world works are all we have as we read and navigate that world. We cannot simply abandon them lest we have no sense of who we are, no sense of how things work, no sense of what knowledge is or how it is justified. It would be a bit like trying to walk away from your own two feet. On the other hand, certain epistemic beliefs that children develop create impasses to their historical understanding. They can create interpretive parochial presuppositions (e.g., the way I see the world is how everyone sees it, texts mean exactly what they say) that profoundly limit children's and even adolescents' historical thinking capabilities and therefore their understandings. For example, one's ethno-racial background, at least in the United States, has been shown to powerfully and differentially influence how, say, a history textbook or a teacher's lecture are understood.[9] Social class also matters as does memory, collective and/or personal.

* * * * *

In Chapter 1, through talk of domain knowledge and structure, I had already begun to allude to a model for learning in the history domain—specifically in my critique of the history test I invited you to take. Here, I want to expand on those ideas with the foregoing discussion of epistemic beliefs and sociocultural anchors in mind. I intend to lay out the model as I conceive it and describe its constituent parts, and show how those parts fit together to overcome unproductive beliefs in ways that produce deeper historical understanding. Along the way I want to suggest how learners can progress from being novices to being reasonably competent. I can then use this model to tease out historical thinking properties that contribute to understanding and that therefore can become the focus of assessments.

Not everyone will necessarily agree with all aspects of my treatment of this model. But it will serve my more specific purpose of making the case for more useful assessment tasks (Chapter 3) and methods for interpreting the evidence of competence (or lack thereof) they generate (Chapter 4).

Historical Thinking

What the body of research on history teaching and learning suggests is that students need to be invited to investigate the past themselves, to focus their efforts on learning the practices that appear to produce the deepest understandings. For better or worse, the model inheres in the community of historians and the practices they employ. We can think of what they do as a form of expertise to which novices can gradually be acclimated on their way toward competence.[10] That cognitive competence is designed to allow for a historical consciousness that is deep enough to overcome the limits of intuitive but counterproductive epistemic beliefs and the parochialism and intolerance that often accompany personal, everyday sociocultural moorings.

The cognitive learning model I sketch here is derived especially from expertise studies, and from their applications among K–16 students. By extension, these studies have profound implications for how teachers would engage students in classroom settings. If the research teaches us how children best learn history on their way to becoming competent historical thinkers, then it stands to reason that teaching practices would align with the model that research describes. For now, the issue of teaching practices will reside in the background of the way in which I describe the cognitive learning model.[11] Nonetheless, the degree to which the learning model, teaching practices, and assessment approaches align allows for assessment data (i.e., evidence of students' growth along the learning trajectory specified in the model) to be interpreted in ways that can provide diagnostic feedback about teaching practice and its successes or shortcomings. As noted, careful alignment is a key characteristic that underpins what follows and I return to discuss it in the final chapter.

The model is idealized. By that I mean it represents an ideal picture of movement from a lack of understanding of particular features of the past to a much deeper understanding. The process of asking questions, addressing them through the exercise of working with organizing concepts and reading and thinking strategies, developing interpretations, and arguing them out (orally and/or in writing) sits in between weak and deep understandings. Because students need to learn this process over time—to do history, as it were—and because students themselves vary considerably one from another, any number of cognitive impasses and sidesteps can occur along the way that vary from the ideal model. The ideal model simply points in a useful direction and helps us know what to do when things get off track.

Questions

Without questions, there isn't much need for serious thinking. Without thinking, there is little understanding. Therefore, developing deeper historical understanding begins with rich questions. What was Harry Truman thinking when he chose to unleash the power of the world's first functional nuclear weapon? Why was a shooting incident in Boston in 1770, one that left five Bostonians dead, portrayed as a "massacre," and by whom and to what effect? What caused the wild growth of American suburbs in the 1950s? Why was so much energy expended to drive the native tribes from their traditional homelands in the American southeast, and who benefited most from their removal and why? An interesting puzzle troubles the process of knowing how to ask these kinds of rich questions, as opposed to questions such as, When did the United States enter World War I? Or, Who was the 16th president of the United States? Apple's handy "friend" Siri (and whomever her eventual successors become) can answer these latter questions in six seconds or less. But try asking her the former questions.

The puzzle pivots on the requirement of already possessing a relatively deep historical consciousness in order to come to the former questions. Students of history do not just wake up one morning knowing how to ask powerful questions of the past. Reading history textbooks, although it might help, does not necessarily result in the capability of enhanced question asking. To put it colloquially, you need to know a lot of history to know how to ask good historical questions. But where is that knowledge to come from? For over 100 years in public schools in the United States, the assumption was that if you simply told students what the past meant, what had effectively occurred, they would learn it and eventually develop into good historical investigators, armed with good questions. We have no data to bear out utility of this assumption and in fact plenty of evidence that the process of learning history simply does not work that way.

The history student cum historical investigator must trek through a process of learning to ask less robust questions initially, acquiring a cognitive tool set for addressing them, learning how those initial answers only then beg deeper historical questions, asking and addressing those deeper questions, and so on. Rich question-asking capability becomes an artifact of asking, investigating, and addressing historical questions in an iterative and generative cycle that, very importantly, takes place in the presence of a more knowledgeable other who can guide and model how it works, how historical knowledge gets built up in ways that enables richer question asking. A good metaphor for describing this is an apprenticeship.

All of this means at least two key things. First, novice learners are unlikely to know enough to ask deep historical questions and therefore will frequently posit what seems trivial or inappropriate to knowledgeable history teachers.[12] And second, this moment becomes the occasion to begin shaping the process of learning how to ask and then address questions, rather than a cue to tell a "hi-story" that turns the novice investigator into a silent, passive accumulator of teacher and textbook narrative on the assumption that question asking will spontaneously appear one day, perhaps when the student is in college.

If historical understanding depends on a historical thinking toolkit and question asking is a pivotal feature of that toolkit, novices need practice asking the questions and flexing their cognitive muscles to address them. Students operating as persistent historical investigators could not be better preparation. Historical questions come first and someone has to guide students in learning how to ask big, meaty, significant ones. Then the guide has to supply the cognitive toolkit for addressing and answering the questions, many of which cannot be answered definitively. This makes things difficult, but not impossible. For some, that challenge of indeterminancy is enough to provoke almost inexhaustible curiosity and interest.[13] What a fantastic way to procure engagement.

So what is this cognitive toolkit? In short, it is a set of strategic and skilled practices that are allied with a series of concepts that link back to rich historical questions, and thus direct the toolkit's use. In this sense, questions function a bit like a blueprint. As I have said, without the toolkit, answering the questions and attaining deep historical understanding as a result is likely to be impossible. And as we just saw, historical questions demand a toolkit if they are to be addressed and understanding is the endgame. The toolkit is indispensable; the more detailed the kit, the deeper the understandings that are possible. So specifically, what are the *tools* and what are their allied *concepts*? Let's begin with the concepts first.

Historical Concepts

In some of the research literature, these concepts are referred to as second-order ideas or procedural concepts because they are allied to the procedural moves and strategies historical investigators make and use as they attempt to answer questions. It is important to note that these concepts do not inhere in the past itself. Investigators effectively invent them and impose them on the past to bring some order to its broad temporal scope and complex, unwieldy characteristics. Some of them function like literary metaphors.

Second-order concepts of the procedural sort include, for example, evidence, accounts, decline/progress, change/continuity, causation, historical significance, historical context, and human agency. Evidence is one of the more crucial of these procedural concepts and it powerfully influences a raft of strategic maneuvers investigators make. Knowing what evidence is in history and how to use it makes no sense without questions, which, to repeat, is why questions come first. Novices typically hold no solid sense of the concept of evidence for their study of the past. They must learn about it explicitly as early as possible. Evidence is probably the most important procedural concept that is initially required. Because evidence derives from accounts (texts, broadly defined), the concept of accounts typically must be paired with the concept of evidence.[14]

Historical context is also critical because evidence and accounts must be situated within the context in which they appear. The concept of agency flows from context. As soon as evidence, accounts, context, and agency appear, concepts such as progress/decline, change over time, and causation begin to play organizational roles. How they are wielded by investigators and to what end depends on the role they play in thought processes. This is where the cognitive, strategic aspects of the toolkit come into force.

Novices must learn through their apprenticeship how to understand these concepts in history-specific ways. This is where their intuitive epistemic beliefs and sociocultural anchors are most likely to create impasses and block progress. For example, young history students are rather quick to judge the human agents of the past by contemporary technological achievements and standards of justice, normative codes, and accepted behaviors. Therefore, if the historical question involves attempting to make sense, say, of the nomadic lives of Plains Indians in the United States, young students judge them to be strange and perhaps ignorant of taken-for-granted assumptions about domesticated life and home building. Plains Indians, after all, dragged their "houses" around behind them. In such cases, some kids dismiss these Indian tribes as not worth understanding, "too dumb" to learn how to construct solid, permanent shelters.

To borrow another Indian example, when kids begin to learn about the 17th-century figure Pocahontas, they are often baffled. She makes no sense to them because she simply does not conform to the contemporary Disney version they have all seen, nor does John Smith for that matter. Understanding grinds to a halt in these cases. You can easily think up any number of variations on this problem. Learning to place past events *in the context* of when, where, and how they occurred becomes crucial to overcoming these sorts of cognitive impasses.

Sorting out what is historically significant in the past, what constitutes progress as opposed to decline, how some events cause certain effects but not others—all are initially approached by novices from their intuitive, taken-for-granted contemporaneous beliefs about the world. These beliefs, more often than not, block historical understanding precisely because 200 or 300 years ago was not altogether like today. Significance is what matters to a child here and now. Progress is what makes the child's life seem "better" today. And effects often have very clear causes; for example, I tell a lie, get caught out, and am punished.

To a student investigating the past, these second-order concepts hold counterintuitive meanings that an apprenticeship process is designed to overcome. Why? Understanding these concepts in what I am calling history-specific ways is pivotal to making sense of the past. The concepts cannot be allied to the strategic part of the toolkit effectively without the development of alternative, counterintuitive definitions for them. That's what makes them difficult to learn. Therefore, they need to be taught explicitly. However, it is best to work on them in the context of an investigation driven by historical questions. There they arise quite naturally because intuitive, novice-like use of the concepts impedes understanding. The wrinkled faces and odd looks signal breakdowns. It is here that good guides see fertile teachable moments.

Cognitive Strategies

Where history-specific second-order, procedural concepts of the sort I have described meet the landscape in which they are exercised—in answering rich historical questions, for instance—cognitive strategies and skills (automatized strategies) join in. The investigator:

- begins to *read residue* (e.g., accounts) from that past;
- identifies what type of accounts they are (*identifies*);
- locates from whom an account comes (*attributes*);
- *assesses* that author's perspective;
- historically *contextualizes* what she reads;
- determines whether that residue *constitutes evidence* for answering questions;
- ultimately *judges the reliability* of accounts for answering questions; and
- attempts to *corroborate evidence* from accounts in order to create answers to the questions posed.

The exercise of the toolkit begins with reading. But notice that the reading is intertextual. In fact, as we have seen, even if the learner (novice or expert, it doesn't matter) chooses to read only one text/account in order to answer her historical question, that text transacts with the text of the world she already holds in her head (her ontological, epistemic, sociocultural anchors, the ones that frame the story in her head she tells about who she is in the world and what that world is like). So there are always at least two texts in play, and often many more than that—thus the intertextuality. This makes reading in history a complicated endeavor that requires some specialized intertextual reading strategies.[15] The strategies of identifying, attributing, assessing, contextualizing, constituting evidence, judging reliability, and corroborating evidence across accounts become crucial to historical understanding.

Young learners, once they have become fluent and functional readers, typically begin learning to develop comprehension and comprehension-monitoring strategies such as looking for a paragraph's main idea, re-reading when meaning-making breaks down, summarizing, and the like. These can be generally useful strategies. But in an always already intertextual world, they are insufficient. This is where history-specific strategies such as the aforesaid become so important. And they must be learned and therefore taught explicitly. Again, learning them in the context of the investigative process is best, not in a routinized and decontextualized way beforehand where they seldom make much sense.

Competence employing these intertextual, history-specific reading, analyzing, and thinking practices can lead to the development of initial interpretations of the past, or in other words, answers to the questions being posed. The stress in doing history is that interpretations must flow out of where and how the evidence preponderates. An interpretation can be thought of as a claim to understanding. That claim must have warrants. Warrants are constituted by the evidence. Countervailing evidence must also be taken into consideration and treated with respect to the claims. In the community of practitioners of history, peers, who have also examined the evidence, judge the adequacy of the claims to understanding (interpretations).

Some researchers who have studied the development of reading in the context of education refer to these forms of reading as disciplinary literacies.[16] Understanding in a discipline such as history is dependent on learning to read in discipline-specific ways. This kind of learning can begin relatively early, in the later elementary grades, where the focus in the curriculum shifts more toward learning in subject matters. It then continues on into middle school and can be developmentally honed in high school. Literacy gradually shifts away from learning how to read, developing fluency, cultivating strategies to monitor one's own reading practices, and developing capabilities to fix comprehension breakdowns and toward constructing in the later grades the kinds of literacies and practices I have been describing.

As I observed in Chapter 1, the ELA Common Core Standards, for example, anticipate this progression in types of literacy practices. By the late elementary grades, the ELA indicators point to the need for students to begin working, for instance, with the concept of evidence in analyzing texts. By the middle and high school grades, as we saw, the indicators have fully shifted to forms of discipline-specific literacies. If these standards are followed carefully and the assessments that measure them are aligned, developmental literacy practices within disciplines will move from the generic to the specific rather rapidly, making new demands on students and teachers. However, despite these demands, such changes hold out hope that historical understanding will be enhanced because students become more accomplished readers (and writers) within the context of the subjects that they are studying, such as history.

Reading accounts from the past and systematically analyzing how these accounts frame potential responses to questions being asked, and then posing interpretations (new synthetic accounts) and arguing about what they mean and/or writing them up is a process that constitutes new historical understandings. Criteria for judging the quality of these new understandings also become important and students must learn about these criteria. Opportunities must be offered to make them explicit. Does the new interpretation address the question(s) being asked? Do interpretations account for all the available evidence? Is evidence cited? Are conflicts among accounts treated? Are warrants for claims to understanding justified and, if so, in what ways? Is the argued interpretation persuasive? Are organizing, procedural concepts employed defensibly (e.g., does the reader carefully source the texts and are texts read in their temporal context)? Does the interpretation attend to the issue of the historical significance of what is being argued? Addressing these questions is a form of assessment. The questions point to criteria (or scoring rubrics—pick your metaphor) for judging understanding *and* the process of getting there.

At this point, I would like to suggest that graphically fitting the pieces of the model I've sketched so far would look something like what you see in Figure 2.1. I include the assessment component to the graphic at the bottom to illustrate its role in feeding back on the processes of questioning, organizing conceptually, thinking-reading-interpreting, and the understandings that emerge.

Historical Understanding

Among novices, the historical understandings that emerge from this process (the large oval in Figure 2.1) will be more or less complete, more or less convincing and persuasive, more or less faithful to the criteria that define competent work in the domain. This should be expected. Learning how to do history in ways that culminate in powerful and deep understandings is a long and complex undertaking. It involves (a) gradually overcoming intuitive but unhelpful epistemic beliefs;

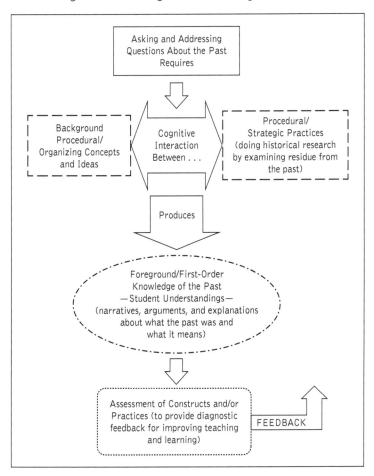

FIGURE 2.1. A Model of Learning in History.[17]

(b) resisting the temptation to judge the past by personal, present-day sociocultural standards; (c) learning to read, analyze, and think carefully, using discipline-specific literacy practices; and (d) building defensible interpretations/understandings that adhere to domain criteria.

To this point, I have postponed mentioning a cluster of historical concepts that are also crucial to the learning process. We can think of these also as types of organizing concepts. However, I would argue that they flow out of the process of attempting to build interpretations and understandings. Rather than being what we are calling procedural concepts, they are names historical interpreters give to events and historical periods in order to mark them off (artificially, some would maintain) from other events and periods. It is the investigator's effort to manage the wide temporal sweep and complexity of the past that emerge from the process of interpreting it. We might think of them as substantive concepts because they attempt to describe the substance of the past.

Some historical concepts, such as the "American Revolution" or "La Belle Epoque," are invented to categorize clusters of events, giving investigators a way to focus their temporal attention. History textbooks make regular use of these colligatory concepts to organize and structure their chronological flow. As such, these concepts are more categorical than procedural. Yet they are linked to the more procedural second-order concepts in that they permit investigators to concern themselves with, say, continuity and change (a procedural concept) during "the Cold War" (a substantive/colligatory concept). Colligatory concepts appear heavily in the histories (understandings of the past) investigators produce. In this sense they can be thought of as first-order because they reside in the foreground of what we call histories. They serve as titles of chapters, as chronological themes, as markers of key shifts in historical time and circumstance.

Many of these concepts that serve to anchor interpretations and understandings are also difficult for learners to master. They appear in synthetic interpretations that students might read as secondary accounts. And not all previous investigators may use a substantive concept in the same way, and/or they might give it shorter or longer temporal sweep. This obviously can be confusing for novices. It becomes important for them to learn explicitly that these terms and concepts are historical investigators' creations, that one investigator may use terms and concepts in slightly different ways than others, and that the novice herself can also invent concepts to categorize elements of her understanding. However, those new inventions must still cohere with criteria within the domain. For example, is the concept employed defensibly?

Does the evidence cited support the use of the concept? Does its use violate the community's widely accepted understanding of how to manage chronology, define historical significance, or describe reasonable parameters of continuity and change?

★ ★ ★ ★ ★

All of these ideas are built up over time as novices learn more about how to make sense of the past and how others have done so before them. It is somewhat akin to an ongoing conversation we in the present have with our ancestors, whether they are earlier historical investigators (Thucydides or Bernard Bailyn) or participants in the developments of the past (Julius Caesar or Dr. Martin Luther King, Jr.). All of this learning begins first with text or story the learner has in his head about who he is in the world. That story begins taking shape early in life, long before school begins.

By the time a novice historical thinker begins learning about the past in a systematic, chronological, and sustained way in later elementary school, that text is already heavily suffused with ideas about history and the past. History learning builds from this text. We can think of this text as the child's memory. It holds personal and collective-culture components. In this sense, historical investigation, or doing history as it were, is also an ongoing conversation between that memory and efforts to bring some discipline to it. We say we value the cultivation of that discipline, which is why we send our children to school to learn about the past, for example. We look to disciplinary practice in history—and I mean this in the sense of harnessing some control over how we think—to provide some guidance. That guidance deepens our understanding and, in so doing, chastens our presentism, parochialism, and cultural intolerance.

However, to make any sort of sense out of whether this mental disciplining process works, whether the model of learning indeed deepens understanding and leavens the effects of present-minded, narrowly parochial, and intolerant judgments about our ancestors (and by extension, each other), we need to assess progress to this end. A relatively clear model helps us identify where we are going, design tasks that therefore can gauge progress, and then interpret what those tasks tell us through powerful assessment-scoring rubrics. Finally, if this all works well, the results provide us diagnostic feedback to reshape—as necessary—how we help learners down the path. If the assessment process is transparent enough, students can get in on it and eventually learn to use that process to assess *their own* learning efforts. Being capable of ongoing self-evaluation is a powerful tool, one increasingly important to life in knowledge-dominant cultures.

Learning to become good at self-assessment can begin in school, and certainly in a subject matter such as history. But as I have tried to show, understanding the assessment triangle and how it works is crucial. It begins with the sort of learning model I have briefly sketched. If we have some sense of how learners' ideas progress and where the impasses are likely to occur as specified in that model, it can point us more directly at the kinds of tasks necessary to gauge development. What those tasks might look like is the subject of the next chapter.

Notes

1 James W. Pellegrino, Naomi Chudowsky, and Robert Glaser (Eds.), *Knowing What Students Know: The Science and Design of Educational Assessment* (Washington, DC: National Academy Press, 2001), p. 3.
2 Ibid., p. 45. My emphasis.
3 By community of practice, I am using the term in the "two-sided" way—a teacher and students working *together* to address questions and solve problems—described by Barbara Rogoff. See her article "Developing Understanding of the Idea of Communities of Learners," *Mind, Culture and Activity, 1* (1994), pp. 209–229.
4 See Joan Wallach Scott, "After History?" Paper presented at History and the Limits of Interpretation: A Symposium (Houston: Rice University, February 1996). Available online at http://www.ruf.rice.edu/~culture/papers/Scott.html.
5 See, for example, Bruce VanSledright and Jere Brophy, "Storytelling, Imagination, and Fanciful Elaboration in Children's Reconstructions of History," *American Educational Research Journal, 29* (1992), pp. 837–859.
6 Roland Barthes, "The Reality Effect," in T. Todorov (Ed.), *French Literary Theory Today: A Reader* (translated by R. Carter, Cambridge, UK: Cambridge University Press, 1968), pp. 11–17.

7 Robert Scholes, *Protocols of Reading* (New Haven, CT: Yale University Press, 1989).

8 Hayden White, *Tropics of Discourse: Essays in Cultural Criticism* (Baltimore: Johns Hopkins University Press, 1978).

9 See, for example, Terrie Epstein, *Interpreting National History: Race, Identity, and Pedagogy in Classroom and Communities* (New York: Routledge, 2009).

10 For more on this point, see Patricia Alexander, "Toward a Model of Academic Development: Schooling and the Acquisition of Knowledge," *Educational Researcher, 29* (2000), pp. 28–33, 44.

11 The model I am proposing, of course, contains affective components (e.g., a learner's visceral reaction to a particularly lurid account of some historical occurrence). How a learner comes to think (cognition) her way through these sorts of reactions on her way to developing deeper historical consciousness is the focus of the model. Therefore, I refer to it as a cognitive learning model because of the *emphasis on learning to think* historically as a means of enabling that deeper consciousness. Affective reactions play roles, but without thinking or reflection on them, there is little further learning. Affect and cognition, therefore, depend on one another for deepening understanding.

12 I am suggesting here that in the early years of becoming a competent historical investigator, it is likely that rich historical questions need to be posed by a more knowledgeable other, the teacher. This is what I mean by modeling the question-asking process. Novices simply do not, at least typically, understand the past deeply enough to ask those rich questions. This does not mean, however, that the questions students propose are *ipso facto* unworthy of consideration. It means rather that they may need to be rephrased in such a way as to make them richer, more powerful. Good history teachers know how to do this. Students' historical questions are also important in that they provide a window onto where they might be on the way to becoming more competent. In this sense, they may hold fertile diagnostic potential. But they still could be insufficient to propel a sustained investigation.

13 In my account of how I taught a group of fifth-grade novices to think historically and learn to investigate the past, I convey the story of two of my students—Jeffrey and Coral—who simply were never satisfied that we could not fully answer the "mystery of the Jamestown 'starving time.'" Independently, without any further prodding from me, they went on an almost endless and difficult pursuit to address the mystery. That investigative curiosity translated into other questions we pursued later in the semester. See Bruce VanSledright, *In Search of America's Past: Learning to Read History in Elementary Schools* (New York: Teachers College Press, 2002), pp. 59–66 especially.

14 Researchers in Great Britain have attempted to study the ways in which young learners make progress in understanding some of these procedural concepts over time. Two key ones they have studied are evidence and accounts. For more detail on the progression models they have developed, see Peter J. Lee and Denis Shemilt, "A Scaffold, Not a Cage: Progression and Progression Models in History," *Teaching History, 113* (2003), pp. 13–23, and Peter J. Lee and Denis Shemilt, "I Wish We Could Go Back in the Past and Find Out What Really Happened: Progression in Understanding About Historical Accounts," *Teaching History, 117* (2004), pp. 25–31.

15 For more on reading historically and its intertextual complexity, see Bruce VanSledright, "Learning With History Texts: Protocols for Reading and Practical Strategies," in Tamara Jetton and Cynthia Shanahan (Eds.), *Adolescent Literacy Within Disciplines: General Principles and Practical Strategies* (New York: Guilford, 2012), pp. 199–226.

16 See, for example, Timothy Shanahan and Cynthia Shanahan, "Teaching Disciplinary Literacy to Adolescents: Rethinking Content-Area Literacy," *Harvard Educational Review, 78* (Spring 2008), pp. 40–59; and Elizabeth Moje, "Foregrounding the Disciplines in Secondary Literacy Teaching and Learning," *Journal of Adolescent and Adult Literacy, 52* (2008), pp. 97–107.

17 A similar version of this graphic is found in Bruce VanSledright, *The Challenge of Rethinking History Education: On Practices, Theories, and Policy* (New York: Routledge, 2011), p. 158.

3

MAPPING ASSESSMENT TASKS TO THE LEARNING MODEL

It might be good here to provide a classroom illustration to contextualize the processes of learning (and by implication, teaching) that were described in the model in the preceding chapter. From that illustration, I can tease out the kinds of specific tasks that can form the assessment.

Assessment tasks are context specific. In some investigations, certain procedural concepts come to the surface and predominate over others. The age of the students also matters, as does how long they have been studying history, in what ways, and how that previous study has affected their understanding of the conceptual, procedural, and strategic range. In other words, it matters what all is in their cognitive toolkits. And who they are also matters, as I noted in describing the learning model.

Finally, it is important to understand that a single assessment, if it is to be given within the typical contextual constraints of schooling (e.g., the standard 50- to 55-minute class period), cannot assess at once every concept, strategy, and understanding in play. Choices must be made about what to focus on. This is why an illustration can be useful in making sense about how to set the tasks.

There are a wide variety of different illustrations I could pose. Anything from the past that lends itself to asking and addressing rich and meaningful historical questions would suffice. The one I wish to use here involves a 2-day investigation into Truman's decision to drop the world's first atomic bomb on Japan near the end of World War II. In most American history curricula, this decision is treated in secondary school. The decision ushered in the nuclear age. It set the stage for the long Cold War that followed. All the dominant high school history textbooks devote at least some attention to it. It surfaces in most standards documents. Many historians consider the decision to be of powerful historical significance because of the way it reshaped thinking about how the postwar period evolved. The arrival of the nuclear age touched almost every aspect of life for the Americans, Soviets, Chinese, Japanese, and almost every other person on the planet ever since. Historical investigators have repeatedly asked, "So what was Truman thinking when he made that profound and fateful decision?" They have also debated the answer. A number of interpretations and schools of thought have emerged since 1945. Some have centered on military considerations, others on political, sociocultural, and moral ones.

The choice of Truman's decision and the focus on the question "What was he thinking?" serves a number of different purposes here. Because the question is such a rich one, it seems like a perfect opportunity for a historical investigation. It would also appear engaging for adolescents in that it invites a look into the mind, a process many of them have already begun through introspection and psychological analyses of peers' and parents' behaviors and personalities.

Furthermore, because understanding Truman and his decision is complex, it does not reduce to some neat and tidy "correct" interpretation, as is the case with so many things in the study of the past. As such, it allows for students to exercise considerable cognitive strategizing as they work through a number of different avenues toward making sense of the decision and the changes it provoked. That strategizing—or thinking historically—then opens up the possibility for creating assessment tasks that gauge where students are along the progression from being novices to becoming more competent. And since multiple ways of understanding the decision are possible, this offers further opportunities to assess growth in interpretive capability vis-à-vis the types of criteria that are characteristic of practices within the disciplinary community. Again, the word *disciplinary* here, by my lights, refers to disciplined thinking of the sort I have already described with respect to the learning model. Investigative practice brings mental discipline, or the power to successfully manage and self-assess one's own thought process. In effect and from a wider perspective, the assessment tasks provide a window onto the development of such mental discipline from within the frame of a common school subject.[1]

An Investigative History Lesson: What Was Truman Thinking?

Imagine a secondary U.S. history classroom context—say, high school level, maybe tenth or eleventh grade in an American school. The teacher, Ms. Beard, has a deep background in American history, specializing in 20th-century developments and World Wars I and II, and the Cold War in particular. Ms. Beard has been teaching for 7 years. She has slowly honed this lesson on Truman since she began teaching. She has found that the question "What was Truman thinking?" has worked well as a frame for exploring the ending of World War II and the beginnings of the Cold War. In that sense, it functions as a transition from one to the other. She has found that if she handles her pedagogical moves successfully, it does much to deepen her students' thinking and understanding capabilities. It typically takes about two class periods to complete.

A Lesson in Two Parts

The effort to make full sense of Truman's decision involves, in part, understanding his thinking *before* he chooses to use the bomb. After all, such a weapon had never been used. As a result, the lesson, Beard thinks, can and should be separated effectively into two parts. The first set of sub-questions then hinge on asking what Truman knew about those atomic weapons prior to the Hiroshima bombing on August 6, 1945 (the bombing of Nagasaki occurred three days later). Did he fully understand the devastation they would cause? Did he comprehend the death and other kinds of casualties that would ensue? What sort of knowledge of the nuclear impact did he have and from what sources? What were his intentions in choosing to use the weapons? What did he think about the possibilities of realizing those intentions? How did he feel about the moral implications? What does he tell us, if anything? If nothing, how might we otherwise "get inside his head," so to speak? What would be the evidence for making claims to understanding him?

The second half of the lesson focuses on the aftermath. A somewhat different set of sub-questions frame that part of the investigation because the bombs' effects are revealed to Truman (and eventually the world). Does he explain why he made the decision? If so, what are his rationales? Does he confirm (or not) that his intentions were met? What sorts of interpretations does the evidence elicited from various accounts allow us to argue about his thinking?

Given these sets of questions, a number of procedural concepts rise to the forefront. One obvious candidate would be causation: effects, causes, consequences, and additional effects and repercussions. Historical context is another, for it is important to understand Truman on his own terms in the context of the ending of World War II, securing a peace and reimagining a reconfigured world with only two real "superpowers" remaining, pitted in many ways against each other. Truman's world was different from that of Beard's students—she knows this and seeks to use the lesson to stress how historical understanding depends on the appropriation of sensitivity toward that difference—contemporaneous rules, norms, and thinking may not fully apply. A third concept is the idea of historical significance, especially relevant here since the ushering in of the nuclear age has such immediate and far-reaching outcomes. Other procedural concepts include evidence and accounts since these are critical to building a case for making sense of Truman's thought processes.

Since questions and procedural concepts are in play, cognitive strategizing must follow. So, the entire toolkit—careful reading of accounts, analyzing, sourcing, and corroborating evidence on the way toward constructing defensible interpretations—must be deployed by students. As such, the lesson appears to be a poster child for teaching about (a) questioning; (b) procedural, organizing concepts; (c) cognitive strategies; and (c) evidence-based interpretation construction (i.e., understanding). And as we will see, it also creates a number of opportunities for Beard to assess students' progression in learning to reason. In short, it is an apprenticeship in learning to think historically in ways that promote deeper understanding, one around and through which she can create powerful, diagnostic assessment tasks. Beard tries to build all her lessons and units using this approach.

Sequencing, Sources, and Summation

In order to proceed, Beard must mine the archive for accounts that her students can read and study. These serve as the raw materials of the lesson sequence. The lesson's first part requires a set of accounts that predate Truman's decision, one he made in July on his return trip from the Potsdam Conference. He learned then from the military that a test weapon had successfully been exploded in the desert of the United States. The military assured Truman that the remaining two atomic weapons in the U.S. arsenal could be deployed almost immediately.

At the Potsdam Conference in July, the United States and China demanded an immediate surrender by the Japanese, telling them that if they resisted, "complete and utter destruction" would follow, without specifying the form in which that would take.[2] There was no response, despite the fact that the United States had been carrying out heavy Dresden-like firebombings of Japanese cities for months, particularly Tokyo, resulting in severe devastation and loss of life. There was talk among U.S. military leaders of the necessity of invading the Japanese mainland to force surrender. Experts debated the number of American casualties likely to result if that invasion were to be undertaken. As commander-in-chief, Truman would have been party to all this information. But what did he know about the bomb and its effects? And would he have been privy to that information? Would its use be enough to prompt Japanese surrender?

Before Beard launches students into a consideration of these questions via an analysis of some surviving print accounts, she harnesses their attention by displaying a set of 8–10 images of the aftermath of the Hiroshima bombing on her classroom Smartboard. She draws these from a *Time* magazine photo essay that appears online at http://www.time.com/time/photogallery/0,29307,2012653,00.html. Several of them are disturbing. They display not only the geographical destruction of the bomb but the human physical consequences as well: heat and radiation burns, scarring, and the like. One image shows a shadow on a stair step where someone had been sitting as the bomb exploded, vaporizing the person and leaving only the human shadow behind. The room is usually entirely silent during this photo essay tour. Sometimes groans of astonishment are audible. Altogether conscious of the luridness of the images, Beard asks, "How could anyone do this?" Silence. That question and subsequent silence allows her to establish some very brief, preliminary historical context before she poses her range of questions and sub-questions about Truman's thinking. Then it's on to reading and analyzing accounts.

Beard drew most of the written/print accounts she uses to address the questions she poses from a website called the Atomic Archive (www.atomicarchive.com). In the website's "Library," under the "Historical Documents" link, are a number of digitized papers spanning initial efforts to develop a nuclear weapon, the Manhattan Project, and the dropping of the bombs, as well as the Cold War period that followed. From the section titled "The Manhattan Project," Beard selected seven documents that would assist her students in wrestling with the questions that framed the first part of the lesson:

*   Einstein's Letter to Roosevelt (1939)—details developments in atomic weapon construction
*   Frisch-Peierls Memorandum (1940)—bomb development progress
*   The MAUD Report (excerpts, 1941)—update on then-present knowledge, including speculation on bomb's destructive potential
*   Chicago Scientists Poll Results (1945)—addressed to A.H. Compton; consensus commentary on how to use the weapon, including the view that Japan should initially see a demonstration of its destructive power
*   Secretary of War, Stimson Diary Extract (July 24, 1945)—commentary on the possible negative consequences of bombing Kyoto, including worry over Japan possibly surrendering to the Soviets instead of the United States in that event

- Memo to General Spaatz (July 25, 1945)—from Thomas Handy, notifying Spaatz of the nature of Air Force readiness to drop the bombs
- The Potsdam Declaration (July 26, 1945)—definition of surrender terms for Japan.

Beard's students also had access to the standard textbook treatment of the lead-up to the Hiroshima bombing. She directed them to it as a means of establishing a timeline should students become confused about historical sequence. She also explained that there were additional accounts on the Atomic Archives website that they could consult on their own if they were interested.

Students would work in small groups, carefully reading and analyzing the documents. Their task was to turn, if possible, these accounts into evidence for answering the Part 1 questions she had posed. She would move around the room, sitting in on discussions, monitoring reading and thinking practices (as reflected in discussions), and addressing student questions that related to the documents. In this sense she was simultaneously a more knowledgeable other and an active learning-community participant.[3] Following this collective practice, Beard would halt group discussion, ask for attention at the front, and begin asking groups to respond to the initial questions posed. She would record comments on the Smartboard as well as require students to defend their conjectures about what Truman knew by citing the accounts from which they were drawing their evidence.

The discussion would typically take some time. Each group would offer its conjectures and defend them, as well as dispute the claims of other groups if differences emerged. And differences often emerged. Students typically disagreed about how much Truman actually knew. Part of what provoked these disagreements hinged on a debate about the degree to which Truman had been fully briefed about the reports and information regarding the bomb prior to his decision. Beard noted that, yes, certain assumptions had to be made since it was not clear from the accounts how privy Truman had been to all of the available knowledge about the bomb. Beard noted that it was customary for a president, as commander-in-chief, to be fully briefed on a regular basis. As such, it would be reasonable to conjecture that Truman knew as much, perhaps more, than her students now knew before he decided to use the bomb on Hiroshima. With that, the class moved on to Part 2.

Beard used the same website to select five documents, four of which were from Truman himself. One account was a secondary source that explained two reasons for Truman's use of atomic weapons. To these she added an excerpt from a famous essay penned by international relations historian Barton Bernstein, published in 1995 in the journal *Foreign Affairs*. Bernstein places Truman within the mental *zeitgeist* of the Roosevelt administration's faith in using the bomb, that the enormous cost of its development would, in part, have been squandered if the weapons were not used. The political costs of not using them, particularly if the war became even more protracted, were not something the Roosevelt administration, the one Truman was a part of and later fully inherited when Roosevelt died, would have tolerated. In short, Truman simply followed a policy direction that had been set in motion long before. The moral question of killing "innocent Japanese civilians" *en masse* was not something Truman pondered much in making his decision. In Bernstein's assessment, Truman harbored no reservations about killing Japanese people given Pearl Harbor, the Bataan Death March, and other acts of wanton aggression the Japanese had perpetrated during the war.

Beard's list of documents included:

- Truman and the Bomb, a Documentary History (n.d., edited by Robert H. Ferrell; from the Truman Library)—suggests that the cost of invading mainland Japan and retribution for Japan's war barbarities were the principal factors in the decision
- White House Press Release on Hiroshima (August 7, 1945)—description of the process of developing the secret bomb used on Hiroshima, and justifying the action because Japan did not surrender as demanded by the Potsdam Declaration
- Truman's Message to Congress on the Atomic Bomb (October 3, 1945)—a plea to Congress to assist in developing domestic policies for control of nuclear weapons

- Truman's Reflections on the Atomic Bombings (January 1953)—recollections of developments leading to the decision, especially noting his worry about Russia's invasion of Japan and to whom Japan would surrender
- Harry Truman, Excerpt from a Letter to the Federal Council of Churches of Christ (several days after Nagasaki bombing, 1945)—reinforces the retribution rationale
- Barton Bernstein (Excerpt from article in *Foreign Affairs*, Issue 1, 1995, p. 139).

The class followed the same procedures as with Part 1 of the lesson. The task this time was to draw from the accounts, many now from Truman himself, to build an evidence-based argument that answered these questions: What was he thinking? What were his reasons?

What typically emerged from discussions that followed the readings were claims that Truman possessed multiple reasons for using the bomb. The first, and a popular one in textbooks, was that Truman sought to end the war as quickly as possible to spare more U.S. military casualties. Beard labeled this the "military rationale" (in effect a substantive, first-order idea). The second turned on the retribution argument, labeled by Beard as the "moral-retribution rationale." The third was a political argument—that Truman more than anything else feared a Soviet invasion from the north and a rapid Japanese surrender to the Soviets rather than the United States. This would allow the Soviets to set the terms of surrender, something Truman desperately wished to avoid. Students making this argument frequently quoted from Truman's 1953 recollections. Beard wrote this one down as the "political rationale."

Typically, students were not sure what to do with Bernstein's claims that Truman was simply following a line of at least implicit policy that called for the use of the atomic weapon as soon as it was ready. They tended to think that the argument did not give enough credit to Truman's own volition and decision-making capacity. Furthermore, they were unsure what to make of the part of the excerpt in which Bernstein states, "America was not morally unique—just technologically exceptional. Only it had the bomb, and so only it used it."[4] Here Bernstein seems to suggest that the use of the bomb was inevitable, at least to the extent that it became an option for any belligerent during the war period, be it the United States, Japan, Germany, Great Britain, the Soviet Union, or whomever. (Beard labeled Bernstein's argument the "inevitability thesis.") By 1945, World War II atrocities on all sides had effectively reshaped the world's definition of wartime morality. Beard's adolescents seemed unwilling to accept what they thought of as too heavy a dose of cynicism permeating Bernstein's claims.

Beard's Goals With the Lesson

Goals frame pedagogical moves and student activity, and the assessment tasks that follow. Beard appears to be working from the cognitive model I've already sketched. Questions shape the investigation. Account analysis and the requirements to generate evidence-based interpretations as a response to the questions put procedural concepts and the cognitive toolkit in play. The interpretations themselves reflect students' growing historical understandings. Assessment practice attempts to get some purchase on the degree to which the process cultivated deeper capabilities in each part of the model: (a) question-asking, (b) first-order and procedural concept use, (c) cognitive-strategy employment, and (d) understanding development.

So what are the specific goals in play here? For Beard, the question-asking portion of the model receives short shrift. She continues to prefer to pose the historical questions she wants her students to investigate. Later in the semester, she foregrounds the question-asking process after she has modeled it over many units and lessons. However, she is very interested in developing her students' capacity to work with a number of procedural concepts in this lesson sequence. Accounts, evidence, historical contextualization, causation, and historical significance rise to the top, while significance's cousin, change/continuity, and another concept, human agency, play important but secondary roles. Beard has realized that it can be tricky to thoroughly teach and then assess all procedural concepts in each unit. So, she uses the topical matter of her units to focus only on several key procedural concepts in each. Because most of her units make use of accounts (multiple) to address questions that in turn potentially transform accounts into evidence, accounts and evidence play recurring and vital roles in her assessment practices. She fits in other procedural concepts, however, as they become relevant to the nature of the topic.

As the process of thinking historically is engaged in her classroom, the entire cognitive toolkit comes into play. Students must be able to (a) carefully and intertextually read and analyze each account within its historical context (contextualizing); (b) identify what sort of an account each is; (c) attribute them to an author; (d) gauge that author's perspective; (e) judge each account's reliability as evidence (or not) for answering the questions that have been posed; and (f) build, refine, and communicate an evidence-based interpretive response. Each of these five thinking strategies and their ancillary components (e.g., functioning as bridges back to several procedural concepts in play) become foci for the assessment practice.

At this point, and at the risk of being redundant, I want to stress how the foregoing cognitive strategies align with the high school indicators in the history portion of the ELA Common Core. In this way, what Beard is doing with her students meets, and likely exceeds, what the ELA Common Core Standards require Although it might not be her most direct goal, her students should score quite well on tests that measure adherence to those standards and indicators.[5] From this perspective, her practices and the activities in which students engage in her history course provide a type of value-added outcome. On the one hand, they are designed to produce deeper historical knowledge, and on the other hand, they link directly to indicators that deal with language arts and literacy.

As a set of examples, consider again the following cluster drawn from the ELA Common Core Standards document. I drew from this same cluster to make several similar points in Chapter 1.

> RH11–12.1.1. Cite specific textual, visual, or physical evidence to support analysis of primary and secondary sources, connecting insights gained from specific details to a [historical] understanding . . .

RH11–12.3.3. Evaluate various explanations for actions or events and determine which explanation best accords with source evidence, acknowledging where sources leave matters uncertain.

RH11–12.8.8. Evaluate an author's premises, claims, and evidence by corroborating or challenging them with other sources or accounts.[6]

Beard's goals overlap closely with these sorts of literacy indicators. One could argue that her assessments therefore also overlap. This makes sense since the foregoing indicators are definitions of historical literacy, ones Beard must rely upon in order to deepen her students' historical understanding. As we will see, to assess as Beard does is, in part, to assess literacy development in history. Her assessment strategies, therefore, apply well to multiple sets of indicators across different standards documents.

Historical understanding—in this case concerning Truman's thinking and rationalizing about using the planet's first atomic weapon on a largely civilian population and how it reshaped the world—is one of Beard's pivotal goals.[7] Therefore it also becomes a pivotal feature of her assessment. Because this cluster of questions about Truman's decision has also animated the investigations of many others, their conjectures and interpretations also appear on this stage, as we saw in the second part of Beard's lesson sequence. They become integral to the assessment right along with Truman's own accounts of his actions.

It might be fair to ask here whether a more formalized, "paper-pencil-type" assessment is even necessary. Since Beard sat in on each group, listened to discussions of the accounts and the initial building of arguments, and held open discussions during which students put on display their interpretive understandings of the questions, would that not be enough for her to get a good sense of what was happening with her students? I would suggest that the answer is both yes and no. Yes, in the sense that such involvement by Beard in the community of practice does provide some data on what's going on. However, not every student gets an opportunity to speak on every such occasion. This means that it would be more difficult for Beard to gauge progression, say on key procedural concepts, without student articulations. In other words, in such cases data become limited for students who do not speak within earshot of Beard. Additionally, although what students say is valuable in assessing progression, it is but one data point. More data points certainly wouldn't hurt. In this sense, a more formal, diagnostic classroom assessment could help in understanding progression across all students.

Unfortunately, we cannot literally observe thinking and understanding. They are processes and outcomes that are invisible because they take place in the mind, out of direct view. One day we might be able to "see" such thinking in operation in ways that show us exactly how reasoning occurs and understandings are built up. But as of yet, we can only "see" changes in neural activity. We must still interpret this activity as a learning process, and the science of how to do that remains imprecise. We are left with proxies of learning: words on a page written by a student, language expressions uttered during discussions or while reading aloud, selections students make between and among question-response options, and the like. All of these proxies must be interpreted. The closer we can get our assessment tasks to map onto what we anticipate to be excellent proxies of learning, the more confidence we can have in what they tell us. This is what I mean by alignment. Clear goals and targets are crucial.

Reworking Assessment Practices in History

Traditionally, it would be at this point that multiple-choice items, perhaps a fill-in-the-blank exercise, and maybe some true-false items would be employed. Maybe even a short essay. As I have argued, these sorts of exercises frequently produce less useful data points rather than more. Therefore, with the above lesson sequence as context, I want to suggest some different ways to go about producing richer, more useful assessment data.[8]

Upside-down, Weighted Multiple-choice Items (WMCs)

As we saw with the history test from Virginia in Chapter 1, the standard and ubiquitous multiple-choice items contain a prompt and a series of selectable options, commonly four. Students choose one option from the list, blacken one of four bubbles or circle one letter, and move on. Depending on her choice, the student either gets it right or wrong. In a domain such as history, such an approach severely limits the range of possible items that can be defensibly posed. Why would this be so?

Most of the richer understandings in the history domain remain open to debate and ongoing reinterpretation. Truman's rationale for dropping the bomb is a wonderful case in point. Was his motivation primarily retribution for Pearl Harbor, including all the moral implications such an interpretation would elicit? Or was it designed more to force the Japanese to surrender to the United States rather than the Soviets, the "political rationale" in Beard's categorization? Or would it be better to argue, as Bernstein maintains, that Truman's decision was part of a running Roosevelt administration policy, inherited by Truman, that should the bomb become ready before the war was over, it would be used?

Exploring this terrain is complex and it eschews tidy, singular correct responses. Typically designed multiple-choice items simply are not up to the task of dealing with this sort of variability. Those items remain mismatched to the past's complexity and indeterminate nature. If we ask instead *when* did Truman make the decision to drop the bomb, or *what time* did the first bomb detonate over Hiroshima, traditional multiple-choice items work. But asking these latter sorts of questions is simply a bit silly here in the 21st century. As I have noted, Apple iPhone's "Siri" can answer them in less than 10 seconds. A Google search may take 15.

What we really want to know is what the past means and how to interpret its messages, how to read it in ways that broaden our understanding of ourselves in the present. Weighted multiple-choice (WMC) questions can be better harnessed to serve this latter purpose. By calling them upside down, I mean that instead of one correct option, such items present only *one incorrect* possibility (which receives 0 points). The other three options are weighted, commonly with the most compelling possibility receiving 4 points, the next most compelling 2 points, and the third receiving 1 point. A 3–2–1–0 structure is also defensible. By designing the test this way, we retain some scoring efficiencies while assessing much more complex ideas and interpretations. These items also do improved justice to the domain's complexity and better respect the way the past tends to resist our efforts to make definitive sense of it.

So what do these WMC items look like? Let me provide an example that Beard might use with her Truman-decision lesson sequence.[9] In attempting to assess historical understanding, the sort that emerges *as a result of* applying procedural concepts and the cognitive strategies toolkit, she asks a question such as the following.

Based on the way the evidence we examined comes together, we can argue that Truman's *primary purpose* for dropping atomic bombs on Hiroshima and Nagasaki during World War II was to

  a. Avoid a costly and perilous ground invasion of the Japanese mainland

  b. Devastate the kamikaze morale and the arsenal of the Japanese air force

  c. Bring about the immediate surrender of axis powers to allied forces

  d. Assert American military strength in the face of communist expansionism

---

In Beard's weighting scheme, response (b) receives zero points because there simply is no evidence within the documents studied in class that indicates Truman worried about a serious remaining threat from the Japanese air force or their kamikaze strategies. Effectively, that threat had been removed by U.S. war operations through the summer of 1945. Options (a), (c), and (d) are more complex and each can be understood as evidence-defensible responses given what Beard asked students to read and study in class.

Option (c), while not incorrect, is a weak choice largely because it had become clear to Truman, as the accounts attested, that the Japanese seemed to be in no hurry to surrender unconditionally. At Potsdam, the allies demanded just such a surrender and received no reply from Japan. Option (c) receives 1 point in this weighting scheme.

The merits of options (a) and (d) as they relate to Truman's intentions can be debated and have been repeatedly. There is evidence to support both, especially from Truman himself. In the documents and accounts Beard used in class, preponderant evidence favored option

(d) over option (a). In fact, the class discussions, while not fully discounting Truman's worry about a ground invasion, centered more heavily on evidence of his pressing concern over a Soviet invasion from the north, a quick capitulation by the Japanese, and their surrender at the feet of the Soviets rather than the United States. Truman believed he needed to act decisively and quickly, thus forcing the Japanese to surrender to U.S. forces. Given that discussion and evidence preponderance, Beard weights option (a) with 2 points and option (d) with 4. She has toyed with the idea of weighting option (d) with 3 points because both (a) and (d) can be defended, with (d)—the political rationale—still retaining an explanatory edge.

How does such an item work and what does it assess? It is important to realize that an item like this represents a contextually bounded space. The prompt is crucial. In this case, the opening clause—"Based on the way the evidence we examined comes together"—sets the space. It signals the contextual boundaries: what we read and discussed in class and how that discussion led us to understand the way evidence clusters to support one interpretation over others. It works to assess students' command of historical reasoning from evidence obtained from a close examination of accounts. But this item does not ask about nor consider Bernstein's "inevitability thesis" or the "moral-retribution rationale," although those ideas certainly could be built into such an item. Doing so, however, would likely change what the item assesses, shifting it away from reasoning from evidence based on careful reading and a classroom discussion and toward students' opinions about what they imagine to be Truman's primary intention. Beard is less interested in assessing those opinions here. This is why the prompt is bounded as it is.

A second weighted-task illustration from Beard's item cluster assesses for what Truman might have known about the destructive potential of the atomic bomb *before* he made his decision to use it. Given the class readings that Beard selected, it is difficult to determine for certain exactly what Truman knew. However, as Beard had mentioned in response to student questions, it was reasonable to assume that Truman, both as vice president and later as president and commander-in-chief, had been fully briefed about the Manhattan Project and what scientists estimated to be the weapon's explosive power, destructive range, and potential for human casualties. Her item attempts to assess what students understand about that assumption.

This understanding is crucial to how students make sense of Truman's initial thinking. If he knew about the weapon's potential power and likely casualties, how would that figure into the way he developed a rationale for his actions? If he was only partially informed, would it be easier or more difficult to choose? And there could be many possibilities in between these two. Here is the item:

As we discussed in class, it is reasonable to say that, *before* he chose to drop an atomic bomb on Hiroshima, Commander-in-Chief Truman

    a. Had already made up his mind that he would use it if it was ready

    b. Was fully informed of the estimates of the bomb's destructive power

    c. Was so busy planning that he didn't know exactly what would happen

    d. Had been purposely left in the dark by scientists and military advisors

---

Option (a) traffics in Bernstein's interpretation, the inevitability thesis. However, students had not read Bernstein until after they had considered Truman's thinking before he fully knew of the actual effects of using the bomb on a city filled with civilians. In this sense and although not wrong per se, option (a) is less applicable to the prompt than other options. It receives a mid-level weight. There is no evidence to suggest that Truman was denied access to key estimates of the bomb's capabilities. Therefore, option (d) is incorrect and receives zero points.

Option (c) is possible but unlikely, especially given what Beard discussed in class regarding how commander-in-chiefs are typically briefed, especially during wartime. It also receives a mid-level weight. Option (b) is the most defensible choice within the bounded context of the item prompt. In Beard's judgment, it receives the highest weight.

The list of such examples could grow quite long. In the interest of space, I would like to move to exploring how such weighted items can be developed for assessing procedural concepts and cognitive strategies. To illustrate other weighted items that can be created for assessing first-order understandings, I include a small cluster of them in the Appendix along with a brief set of rationales for their weighting structures. In the next chapter, I also explain in more detail about the weighting structures and their rationales, and how to interpret scoring outcomes as evidence of student learning and progressions from weaker to stronger ideas.

As I noted, understandings of procedural concepts and their connected cognitive strategies can also be assessed using such WMC items. Consider this item:

In doing history, investigators often find accounts that contradict one another, even among those that testify firsthand about the same past event. One way of dealing with this problem is to

    a. Build a new narrative from elements of truth conveyed by those accounts

    b. Corroborate the evidence provided by those accounts with other sources

    c. Suspend judgment until a definitive source is found

    d. Focus only on the facts provided by those accounts

The item assesses students' understanding of accounts as evidence for making claims, how "truth" in accounts might be conceptualized if at all, the way corroboration between and among accounts relates to evidence-based claims, and potentially the role facts could play in developing an understanding. In many ways, it is linked to the Truman-intention question, but takes on a more direct procedural, strategic focus. Option (a) implies that it is a relatively straightforward process of separating truth from fiction and/or distortion in accounts. Beard has taught her students that there is nothing straightforward about that process at all. In testimonies about past events, one person's truth ends up being another's lie. It is frequently difficult to tell the difference. Option (d) suggests a similar but somewhat less tricky effort. It is possible to glean a few brute facts from different accounts about the same incident, for instance. However, it remains a tough task to synthesize those few brute facts into a meaningful understanding. Faced with this problem, a student could choose option (c), suspending judgment and embarking on the quixotic search for that definitive source that settles the testimonial dispute.

In history, "definitive accounts" simply do not exist because an author's perspective always comes into play. That perspective may be definitive to that author, but not to other eyewitnesses or interpreters. Of the four options in the bounded frame of this item, option (d) is the least effective approach to making sense of and interpreting contradictory accounts in history. In fact, it blocks interpretive progress. This leaves option (b). It is a synthesis strategy that allows forward progress in interpreting the past. It is rooted in the idea of corroborating testimonies across accounts, of testing how evidence preponderates. This is a key procedural idea that Beard repeatedly stresses and models in class. Therefore, it would receive the top weight, with option (c) receiving zero points and options (a) and (d) receiving in-between weights because they are not "wrong" strategies, just less helpful than the one (b) describes.

In a broader sense, this procedural-concept item also assesses a type of epistemic thinking in history. It goes to the idea that we can make defensible claims about what the past means only to the extent that we can corroborate evidence across accounts. The more we can do this, the less conjectural our claims become. Conjecture may be necessary when the evidence is not readily forthcoming or does not preponderate convincingly in any particular direction. Yet the greater the conjecturing, the more open the interpretation is to alternative and competing versions. Therefore, more powerful epistemic reasoning requires more advanced strategies, such as corroboration.

Here is another example that deals with the second-order procedural concept of contextualization:

Based on our conversations in class and what we learned about good investigative study of people in the past, our interpretations of those people's ideas and actions are best explained

    a. From within the historical context and period in which they occurred

    b. By understanding them based on our present standards of morality

    c. Through imagining what they must have thought and felt

    d. In relationship to what others thought of their behavior

---

Because they are inescapably guided by their understandings of present-day standards and norms concerning appropriate behavior, judgment, and thought processes, students in Beard's class make a practice of regularly interpreting accounts by drawing from such standards. As a result, Beard spends considerable time stressing, for instance, the fact that Truman needs to be understood within the zeitgeist of the World War II era, which preceded full comprehension of atomic-weapon capabilities and consequences. Such understanding is difficult for her students; all they really know is a potentially dangerous nuclear world with its Chernobyls and Fukushima Daiichis. She uses an item such as the one above to assess progression in contextualizing accounts and understandings of them.

Here, option (a) is clearly the answer she is after. Option (b) is what students gravitate toward. Option (c) is a form of contextualizing (e.g., engaging in a type of empathic regard) and so is not inaccurate. However, it is somewhat less clear and precise than option (a), given Beard's classroom use of option (a) language. It is also less sufficient in that empathic regard is but one type of contextualizing practice and, as an effort, it can quickly resort to depending upon contemporary normative standards. Option (d) is another form of contextualization related to corroboration. However, it has distinct limits, especially if what "others thought" is not particularly obvious. Options (c) and (d), therefore, receive mid-level weights, while options (a) and (b) represent the poles in the bounded space of this item.

A wide range of understandings and strategies can be assessed using such WMCs. They also have the virtue of helping teachers better diagnose stumbling blocks in students' historical thought processes. For example, if students persist in choosing the mid-level, weaker options even after the importance of corroboration strategies or contextualization practice have been stressed and modeled, this calls for additional open pedagogical modeling. To gauge change in student thinking over time, similar weighted items that sample, say, the concepts of corroboration, evidence preponderance, and contextualization can be integrated into successive assessments. This gives history teachers purchase on the growth, or the lack thereof, among students over time. If there is evidence for the latter, it suggests a pedagogical and curricular attention and redirection.

What we typically do with common multiple-choice items is lament the fact the students "didn't seem to get it." But because these typical items lack for cognitive progression points (choices are either right or wrong and often assess not much more than reading-comprehension capability), they do little to help teachers know what to do about it. Weighted items—although no panacea because we lack such a cure-all assessment technology at present—do help move in a direction that provides teachers with useful diagnostic tools.

One other benefit that arises from employing WMC items deserves mention. Beard makes a practice of opening up her weighting structures to challenges from her students. That is, she makes her weighting decisions transparent. She then invites her students to argue with her if they believe that an option selected can be defensibly awarded the top number of points, even though she scores it in the lesser range. She requires a strong, evidence-based rationale for making that change.[10] In so doing, she encourages her students to become self-assessors who can unpack weighted items, study the weighting rationales relative to their own choices, and make reasoned claims for alternate interpretations. The practice also reinforces an understanding of the deeply interpretive and sometimes contentious nature of understanding the past, one epitomized by debates within the domain.[11]

Writing Interpretive Essays

Writing is thinking on paper or on screen. Because good writing requires a disciplined display of thinking, it holds the capacity to demonstrate understanding. For this reason it has often held a prominent place in history assessments. Document-based questions (DBQs), for example, have played a time-honored role in attempts to gauge student understanding, from tests in Advanced Placement history courses to the New York Regents exam. And many history teachers have been known to rely on variations of them in their courses. In that sense, such essays are nothing new. However, I would like to explore this approach in more detail with an eye to how they can be used to generate more precise and useful diagnostic evidence of students' historical thinking practices and understandings. Much of achieving that usefulness depends upon not only the kinds of interpretive tasks set by the parameters of the writing prompts, but also the nature of the rubrics used to assess the results. I take up those rubrics in the next chapter. Here I confine my analysis to types of writing prompts.

Question Prompts With Documents. As noted, the DBQ is one of the more familiar assessment writing tasks. Generally speaking, students see several short accounts they are asked to read that offer testimony about or explanations of a historical incident, decision-making process, or the like (there might be infinite possibilities here).[12] These are followed by a writing prompt that asks them to synthesize the accounts and construct an interpretation of the incident or process using those accounts. The quality of the writing and the nature of the interpretation are frequently the subject of scoring.

But how can the ways these tasks are constructed most fruitfully map onto the learning model discussed in the last chapter? If the goal is to assess both thinking practice and understanding of the past, how can a document-based task assess both? Since writing is time consuming and energy and effort intensive, assigning students a raft of such questions (e.g., around Truman's decision to drop the bomb) to more fully map the model's learning goals could be cost prohibitive. So, how could we get the most from a single such writing task? Part of the key to answering these questions hinges on how a prompt is constructed. Let's use the Truman bomb-decision example as an illustration.

It is helpful first to be clear about which types of thinking practices and understandings the writing task will sample. This is an important issue because one writing task is unlikely to be able to sample every cognitive strategy, procedural concept, and interpretive goal contained in the model. Simply put, certain historical subjects, topics, or events lend themselves to assessing particular practices and understandings better than others. Choosing and focusing must occur. In the Truman example, if Beard asks her students to write on the prompt "What was Truman thinking when he chose to use the atomic bomb on Japan?," she is effectively posing a question about causation. In other words, what caused Truman to make the choice he did?

Multiple forms of causation are common. Truman may have considered a variety of different rationales for his choice. Beard's students, therefore, could write essays in which they argued that more than one set of considerations (e.g., ending the war sooner, avoiding political and economic embarrassment at home, following along with the policies of the Roosevelt administration of which he was a part) account for his actions. However, a student might also choose to construct an argument that one particular line of reasoning caused him to choose as he did. A number of possibilities present themselves, unlike the more bounded space created by the prompt of a multiple-choice, weighted item that asks about what caused Truman to think as he did.

The use of evidence and making sense of how that evidences preponderates (corroboration) across the accounts that students examined becomes crucial. For example, if a student chooses to identify and argue for one principal cause (e.g., ending the war more quickly), she must support that thesis by being clear how the evidence points predominantly in that direction and away from alternative theses (e.g., avoiding political/economic embarrassment). This means that she must take into account those other possibilities, note them clearly, and argue convincingly against them. Failure to consider alternative interpretations present in the documentary evidence would allow for others to counter with them, thus reducing the power and persuasiveness of her argument.

Contextualization as a form of historical thinking is also pivotal here. A student needs to consider Truman on his own terms, in the context of this particular mid-1940s period of time. Accusing Truman of making an unconscionable choice, especially given the context of the immoral choices made during World War II on all sides, suggests a degree of disregard for the importance of historical context in understanding and interpreting what Truman was thinking. As such, it signals room for improvement in the capacity to think historically.

Open-ended, interpretive questions such as this Truman example provide powerful opportunities for students to display how they reason historically, interpret the past in ways that make sense, and work from pivotal procedural concepts and cognitive strategies. In that sense, they can serve as important assessment tools for gauging progress in the development of historical thinking and understanding.

Single-Account Interpretation Essays (SAIEs). If the DBQ is perhaps the most familiar type of student writing task in history, it is far from the only one. Since the research makes clear how important reading and interpreting historical accounts is to understanding, open-ended questions can be designed that also assess more directly how that reading and interpreting occur.[13] A writing task could be presented to students in which an account—say, "Truman's Reflections on the Atomic Bombings" (from January 1953)—is provided and students are prompted first to explain how they went about interpreting the account, and second to lay out what the account tells us about what Truman thought his reasons were for his choice to use the atomic bomb while also explaining why they can be considered his reasons.

A series of reading and thinking strategies (e.g., identifying the account, attributing it, assessing its perspective, contextualizing it, looking for evidence that addresses the second part of the prompt) could be listed in a box next to Truman's account. Students would be encouraged to work those strategies into their explanations of first prompt noted above. This could be accomplished in a paragraph or two. The following paragraph or two would be devoted to the second portion. There should be a considerable degree of correspondence between the two parts of the prompt. By that I mean if a student engages with a number of the history-specific reading and thinking strategies listed in the box and can clearly articulate how he employed them, the resulting explanation of Truman's reasoning should reflect that careful reading and thinking. A number of Truman's reasons would be identified (perhaps quoted) and the subsequent explanation for choosing those reasons would make sense given the nature of the account. Such an item gives purchase on the ways in which students read and interpret accounts. Again, how these items are scored matters, and I attend to that issue in Chapter 4.

An alternative approach here might involve posing several related short-answer questions such as: (1) If you were trying to make sense of Truman's reasons for using the atomic bomb on Japan, in what specific ways does this account shed light on them? (2) As a historical investigator, how would you go about interpreting this account? (3) Is this account reliable for making sense of Truman's thinking, and why or why not?

The first question requires careful, contextualized reading and analysis followed by the expression of an interpretation (also addressed by the ELA Common Core Standards). The second question asks the student to make her interpretive, strategic thinking transparent (again, addressed by indicators in the ELA Standards). The third question relates to the idea of evidence and how accounts are judged as reliable (or not) for making evidence-based claims. It is a request for an explanation that includes more precise reasoning about how to interpret accounts than the second question because it asks specifically about making reliability judgments. The rubric would be constructed around these three targets.

Project Presentations. Students can also be asked to construct presentations and design small websites that display how they researched and arrived at interpretations of the historical questions they undertook to address. A response to the question based on the research would constitute students' interpretive understanding. Students could conduct the research collaboratively as well as design the presentation or website.

Like DBQs and SAIEs, such presentations and website development work entails writing, and writing is thinking as well as a means of conveying understanding (or the lack thereof). Carefully constructed rubrics for scoring them can reveal much about learning progressions, especially if multiple similar types of presentations are part of the assessment strategy across a history course. Beard also has found that they are particularly useful in considering historical topics in which a number of pivotal historical sub-questions can be raised and need addressing (e.g., those that surround understanding causes of the U.S. Civil War). Groups are assigned different investigative questions, engage in the research and interpretive work, and publicly present their results on completion via a webpage design or multimedia presentation.

Other Assessment Strategies

Beliefs Questionnaires. What learners believe history is—how it is distinct from the past (or not), how investigators adequately justify their claims about what the past means, and how evidence is marshaled to make claims—all influence how they make sense of history. Learners' beliefs are often counterproductive. For example, studies have demonstrated that young learners in particular see no difference between history and the past, thinking that history is simply a given chronicle of what happened and so is isomorphic with it.[14] Learners can also struggle with what to do with accounts that present conflicting testimony. In those situations, they can resort to the aforementioned naïve idea that an account's author must either be telling the truth or lying.

Both these beliefs (among a number of others) create problems for learning in history because they form cognitive impasses. If an account is either truthful or deceitful, it requires an effort to know the difference if progress in understanding is to be achieved. But often, figuring out precisely that difference is impossible when doing history. When that happens, understanding is arrested. Similarly, if a learner works from the belief that there is no difference between the past and history—that history directly corresponds to the past—her progress toward understanding will be blocked when she discovers that an account omits certain details, as many accounts do.

Learners sometimes have significant difficulty giving up these beliefs. In the case of the truth-lie dichotomy, it holds powerful sway because it is something most young children learn about very early. It shapes a number of their interactions with parents, siblings, and friends from that point forward. However, believing that stories fall into only those two categories makes successfully investigating the past virtually impossible. The idea of an author's perspective coupled with the notion that two people can hold legitimately different and competing perspectives is a much more helpful belief. But to get there requires the learner to go beyond the truth-lie dichotomy. Investigating the past well necessitates belief changes.

At least occasionally assessing beliefs, then, becomes important in history education if teachers wish to understand more about what might be blocking students' progress. Short beliefs questionnaires are reasonably easy to construct, administer, and score. Statements that reflect beliefs, or what I prefer to call epistemic stances, can be listed out. To the right of each statement a four-part Likert scale can be presented

	I strongly agree	I agree	I disagree	I strongly disagree
1. There is no difference between the past and history.	1	2	3	4
2. An account from the past only reflects the perspective of the person who authored it.	1	2	3	4
3. Some accounts do not address the question I am trying to answer and so are unreliable.	1	2	3	4

FIGURE 3.1. Sample Historical Beliefs Questionnaire.

with poles represented by "I strongly agree" and "I strongly disagree." Students can quickly indicate their beliefs by circling which response on the Likert scale represents their position.

Figure 3.1 represents a brief example of what such a questionnaire might look like. It contains only three items. However, adding more statements can increase the questionnaire's reach and diagnostic power.[15] How students respond to these statements, especially if the questionnaire is used periodically across a history course, can yield rich evidence for assessing if and how unproductive beliefs change over time. That evidence can be used to make pedagogical adjustments.

Interest Surveys. Interest in a subject matter has been shown to correlate with increased learning of that subject matter and more subject knowledge tends to increase interest.[16] Keeping track of student interest in history as a subject domain, therefore, tells us something about the likelihood that learning will increase or decline. It provides additional data for making pedagogical decisions especially if otherwise strong interest begins to decline, or if certain students show consistently low interest in what occurs in the history classroom.

It is tempting to simply ask students if they enjoy the course or find history topics interesting. Such approaches are not immune from producing outcomes that predominantly reflect social-desirability effects. A method of avoiding that problem is to ask learners what they do, rather than what they may think or feel. For example, it is reasonable to assume that learners are interested in history if, away from school, they have taken to watching historically themed films or using the Internet to search out additional ideas about a topic they are studying in class, or find historically themed museum exhibits compelling enough to visit them. Parental influence may factor into these activities. But that may actually help increase interest.

Constructing such interest surveys is relatively straightforward and they can be quick to administer and score. Beard uses periodic 5- to 7-item interest surveys. The items include statements that ask students what they do, such as "I regularly watch history-type movies at home or in the theater," "I like to look up additional ideas about the history topics we study in class on the Internet," and "I sometimes visit historic buildings in my community." She provides a 10-point continuum (1 = low interest and 10 = high) in which students place an X along the continuum that reflects a range from "I never do this" (1) to "I do this often" (10). Attempting to avoid an overabundance of socially desirable responses, she explains to students that she does not "grade" these surveys and high or low scores on their face will not impact how they are graded on tests and assignments. Whatever students select on the continuum should be an honest assessment of what they do, not what they think she wants them to do; their time away from school is, of course, their own. Beard is just curious about how her classroom activities may relate to their lives away from school. Students have come to trust her on these claims.

As a result, she obtains reasonably honest responses. The scores tend to correlate with what she observes by way of in-class activity engagement from topic to topic and unit to unit. Some students are perennially bored with school in general. Their interest-survey responses reflect this, as do the ways in which they progress (i.e., glacially) in learning to think historically and understand the past. Beard uses the results as evidence for making choices about how to reach out more intensively to those students in an effort to increase their interest levels, at least in her class. Sometimes her reaching out, especially in personal conversations, reveals that James or Ericka is not actually disinterested; he or she simply does not understand how Beard's classroom is working, feels lost, and is discouraged. The last thing James and Ericka wish to undertake is doing more history away from school. Hence their low interest survey results. This gives Beard a means of better understanding what she can do to help them progress.

★ ★ ★ ★ ★

Two other powerful assessment strategies are worth noting—conducting verbal reports and engaging in analyses of classroom video recordings. However, both require significant time commitments and as such tend to be somewhat impractical. Nonetheless, they can be deeply revealing about the ways students think historically and how they participate in class and respond to investigative activities. For those reasons, these two strategies are worth a brief discussion.

Verbal Reports. Verbal reports have been used by reading researchers to sort through how readers make sense of text as they read, or by other researchers who are interested in understanding how people work their way through complex tasks or problems.[17] If teaching efforts involve helping students think historically, and much of doing so hinges on reading, analyzing, and interpreting historical texts, verbal reports can serve as a useful proxy for elements of that developmental process. One such task could be constructed in which students read multiple, consecutive accounts of a historical incident or decision-making process (e.g., the shootings in Boston in March 1770, General Custer's "Last Stand," what Truman was thinking about when he decided to use the atomic bomb) and talk out loud about what they are thinking as they go. With a recorder running, teachers can obtain a record of what students say they are thinking about as they read, construct ideas, and interpret the accounts (or pictures, paintings, or photographs).

Thinking through and constructing ideas about the past while reading are such common practices among historical investigators that engaging students in such a practice turns out to be yet another fertile way of gathering data about what seems to be going on in their heads as they are trying to make sense of it. A key to assessing changes in students' cognitive capabilities and understandings involves conducting verbal reports over time.

If undertaken properly with as little intervention by the verbal-report administrator (e.g., a history teacher), these protocols are about as close as we can get to "seeing" thought and meaning making in action. It is important to note, however, that a verbal report transcript remains only a proxy of thinking. Certain thinking processes may not necessarily be tapped during a verbal-report protocol. Turning the results into evidence that gauges student historical reasoning still requires inferences about what is happening for the student. Those inferences must be guided by a coding system or rubric that is theoretically defensible and closely linked to the learning model discussed in Chapter 2.

Video Analyses. The second powerful but also time-consuming assessment strategy is to video record classroom activities—say, a discussion of different interpretations of what Truman was thinking. These recordings can later be replayed and mined for what they reveal about the ways in which students express their thinking in class. You are probably saying to yourself, "Well, if I was the teacher, I was there. Why would I need to replay a video to see what happened?" This is a reasonable question.

The advantage of video recordings hinges on the fact that teachers are very busy making a cluster of ongoing pedagogical decisions and moves to keep a lesson flowing as intended. The human mind simply cannot attend to everything at once. Certain details and occurrences are deprioritized and therefore do not lodge themselves in memory in ways that are easily recalled. Video recordings enable a process of examination and assessment after the fact that simply was not available in the moment. As a result, they are deeply useful for reviewing and assessing student activity, contributions, thought processes, and understandings. To maximize their benefit, it again helps to know what to look for. This depends on the learning model and a coding system derived from it.

The Importance of Overlapping Assessment Strategies

By way of concluding this chapter, let me discuss briefly why drawing from a variety of overlapping assessment strategies can be so beneficial for gathering accurate evidence of what is occurring for students. Overlapping here means that the strategies are best used in combinations. This allows for obtaining multiple observation points on the same student learning targets. I have tried to show that different assessment strategies (e.g., WMC items and essays) can measure the same procedural concepts, thinking practices, and historical understandings, but can go about it in different ways.

If we assume that the assessment strategies yield valid data, and my experience with these types of approaches indicates that they do, to generate multiple observation points provides an opportunity to corroborate data. Doing so builds confidence that one can make meaningful, evidence-based claims about student understanding, or the lack thereof. And this is a principal goal in diagnostic assessments—to generate useful evidence upon which sound pedagogical and curricular decisions can be based, ones that continually enhance and deepen learning. This is precisely why they are worth the effort to create well.

To illustrate this point a different way, if two different items or tasks that are designed to observe the same understanding produce quite contrary results, then either something odd is happening for a student (e.g., misreading), or there is something amiss with one or both items/tasks (e.g., one is improperly aligned with the learning model). This is a signal to reassess the student's understanding and/or to reexamine the items.

In either case, using overlapping assessment strategies increases the likelihood that the results will demonstrate greater degrees of validity (measuring the concept or idea that was designed to be measured via the learning model) than if only one task or item was employed. Strong evidence follows from greater validity. All of this depends, of course, on how items and tasks are interpreted and by what criteria. Just as assessment strategies need to align with the learning model, interpretation criteria need to carefully align with tasks and items.[18] This is the subject of the next chapter.

Notes

1 Of course, I am assuming that the harnessing of mental discipline is a valuable accomplishment, one that helps us navigate a complex world. I am trying to show here how little I am interested in teaching students to do history because I think they all should become historians someday. I am much more committed to the ways in which history, as just one school subject, can be mobilized to help students take charge of their lives and become responsible, engaged, and above all thoughtful citizens of the planet. Learning to become disciplined historical thinkers is but one path, albeit a powerful one, toward this goal.

2 At Potsdam, Truman did hint to Stalin that the United States possessed weapons with unparalleled firepower, again without specifying exactly what those weapons were. He seemed to be saying that the United States controlled a whole arsenal of these weapons, when it turned out they held only three at that point, one of which was detonated as a test prior to the consecutive Hiroshima and Nagasaki bombings. For his part, Stalin noted that the Soviets were planning to invade Japan from the north no later than mid Fall 1945. However, on August 8, 1945, the Soviets declared war on the Japanese and invaded Manchuria, then controlled by the Japanese. This came as a surprise to Japan's military leaders, who now saw an imminent threat coming not only from the Pacific in the form of the U.S. military, but from the north and west as well.

3 For more on the importance of this role, see Barbara Rogoff, "Developing Understanding of the Idea of Communities of Learners," *Mind, Culture and Activity, 1* (1994), pp. 209–229.

4 See Bernstein's *Foreign Affairs* article, p. 139.

5 Of course, this assumes that the eventual assessment strategies employed to measure such ELA indicators are actually aligned with those indicators. Given the history of testing practices in the United States, this outcome is not necessarily a given. Part of what I am trying to show here is that the types of assessment strategies Beard uses are deeply relevant to and applicable for assessing ELA indicators.

6 These ELA CC Standards and their history strands are available online at http://www.corestandards.org/the-standards/english-language-arts-standards.

7 The ELA Common Core Standards are silent on the types of first-order substantive understandings students are to develop at the secondary level. This makes sense since they are principally focused on the development of disciplinary literacies—reading, writing, and communicating ideas in subject areas such as history—not on the substantive knowledge students are to

develop. The latter is more the province of the social studies state inquiry framework and state standards documents.

8 My goal here is to provide assessment examples that suggest a range of performance-based, diagnostic alternatives. The ideas that follow are meant to be illustrative, but not definitive. Smart history teachers undoubtedly will have thought up and employed other examples that I do not include.

9 For another set of such items built for assessing student thinking about and understanding of Cherokee Indian removal during the 1830s, see Bruce VanSledright, *The Challenge of Rethinking History Education: On Practices, Theories, and Policies* (New York: Routledge, 2011), Chapter 6 on assessment.

10 Frivolous cases are discouraged. Beard warns her students that unwarranted and unsubstantiated claims for changes may be met with point deductions. Students must do their homework and come equipped with strong arguments rooted in historical evidence. If those arguments are persuasive, Beard awards the highest weight.

11 For example, see the interpretive debate between historians Robert Finlay and Natalie Zemon Davis in the *American Historical Review, 93* (1988), pp. 553–603. See also Allan Megill, *Historical Knowledge, Historical Error: A Contemporary Guide to Practice* (Chicago: University of Chicago Press, 2007), Chapter 6 especially, and David Hackett Fischer, *Historians' Fallacies: Toward a Logic of Historical Thought* (New York: Routledge and Kegan Paul, 1971).

12 I am referring to written accounts here. However, cartoons, photographs, paintings, and charts and graphs could also be used. All these different types of accounts (or depictions) potentially can be transformed into evidence for making claims about what the past means. Which accounts, broadly defined, are decided upon will have to do with what has been studied, what the target concepts are within that study, and what understandings are desired.

13 See, for example, Peter Lee, "Putting Principles Into Practice: Understanding History," in Susan Donovan and John Bransford (Eds.), *How Students Learn: History in the Classroom* (Washington, DC: National Academies Press, 2005), pp. 31–78; Sam Wineburg, *Historical Thinking and Other Unnatural Acts: Charting the Future of Teaching the Past* (Philadelphia: Temple University Press, 2001), Chapter 1; Peter Seixas, "The Community of Inquiry as a Basis for Knowledge and Learning: The Case of History," *American Educational Research Journal, 30* (1993), pp. 305–324; and Stephane Levesque, *Thinking Historically: Educating Students for the 21st Century* (Toronto: University of Toronto Press, 2008), Chapter 2 especially.

14 See Peter Lee and Denis Shemilt, "A Scaffold Not a Cage: Progression and Progression Models in History," *Teaching History, 113* (2003), pp. 13–23.

15 Statements can be expressed both positively and negatively, and some combination of the two is good. Successive versions can switch the positive-negative direction of statements to avoid practice effects—that is, students seeing exactly the same statements each time and "mastering" the questionnaire. It is also worth noting that such questionnaires can be subject to responses that reflect what seems socially desirable in the history course context. In that sense, it may help to provide several lines below each statement and request that students explain briefly why they choose the Likert response that they did.

16 See, for example, Patricia Alexander, Jonna Kulikowich, and Sharon Schulze, "How Subject-Matter Knowledge Affects Recall and Interest," *American Educational Research Journal, 31* (1994), pp. 313–337, and Patricia Alexander, Tamara Jetton, and Jonna Kulikowich, "Interrelationship of Knowledge, Interest, and Recall: Assessing a Model of Domain Learning," *Journal of Educational Psychology, 87* (1995), pp. 559–575.

17 See, for example, K. Anders Ericsson and Herbert Simon, "Verbal Reports as Data," *Psychological Review, 87* (1980), pp. 215–251.

18 See Pellegrino et al., *Knowing What Students Know.*

4

INTERPRETING ASSESSMENT TASKS

What do the observations of student learning via the assessment tasks mean? And what claims about changes in students' historical thinking and understanding can be made from them? To answer these questions, we need interpretation strategies, the third part of the assessment triangle.[1] Interpretation strategies should derive directly from the theory that guides the learning model. As we have seen, that model allows us to create tasks that, with careful attention to the model, map onto it. The tasks then generate data in the form of observations of learning (or the lack thereof). Yet we still need methods for making sense of those observations that point back toward the model if we are to be able to assert reasonable claims, ones that can allow us to diagnose students' learning difficulties and adjust teaching approaches and the curriculum in order to make enhancements.

Interpretation strategies constitute a type of inferencing. We cannot actually observe learning taking place, so to say "observing learning" is a misleading. Learning occurs invisibly inside the minds of students.[2] All we can obtain through the tasks we ask students to undertake are proxies of learning. Therefore, inferencing must occur—that is, interpreting and judging what students appear to tell or show us is going on in their minds. At present, that's as good as it gets. As I have been arguing, our best efforts will depend on having a clear learning model (Chapter 2) that specifies tightly aligned and robust tasks (Chapter 3). Continuing to adhere closely to the model in turn enables sound interpretations of the data those tasks generate.

In what follows, I concentrate on the historical thinking and understanding tasks specified in the last chapter (WMC items, writing tasks, etc.). It is these that require the keenest interpretation strategies and criteria. Generally speaking, I leave aside assessment strategies that focus on obtaining students' self-reports of their own learning (e.g., interest surveys) and approaches with rich potential but lower practical utility (e.g., verbal reports), except to note the role they might play as forms of corroborating evidence. I extend the analysis in this chapter by attempting to demonstrate what sharp rubrics and robust coding systems (as interpretation strategies) can do to help history teachers like Ms. Beard improve on her own teaching practice and speak to the learning opportunities (i.e., curriculum) she makes available to her students. Finally, to provide continuing context, I mostly stick with the specific assessment tasks linked to Beard's lessons regarding Truman's atomic bomb decision.

Revisiting the Learning Model

In order to develop sound and diagnostically useful rubrics and coding schemes for interpreting task data, we need to briefly revisit the learning model, as we did in constructing the assessment tasks themselves. If the goal is to make sense of students' emerging and changing historical-thinking capabilities and understanding of the past, we use the learning model to specify what thinking and understanding mean. Being as precise as possible here is important. However, in an ill-structured, indeterminate discipline like history, that looseness can sometimes defeat our best intentions at achieving precision.

Historical Thinking

Historical thinking begins by asking and addressing historical questions. As I noted, Beard typically models the question-asking process for her students on the assumption that students often struggle to construct the kinds of rich historical questions that animate investigations in the domain. However, she gradually begins to turn question construction over to students as the course proceeds. Beard does plunge her students into the processes of addressing historical questions.

Addressing questions involves applying, often simultaneously, second-order procedural concepts and cognitive strategies. Key procedural concepts include *causation, progress/decline, continuity/change, contextualization, accounts, evidence,* and *perspective.* Being able to simply state a definition of one or more of these concepts can help, but is likely insufficient. It is how students deploy them in practice—perform them as it were—that is of most interest to Beard. They are concepts-in-use, thus the label procedural concepts. Once deployed, they merge with cognitive strategies. Those strategies include careful *reading and analyzing, identifying and attributing* accounts, *assessing* an author's perspective,[3] *interrogating* an author's account, *judging* an account's reliability for providing evidence that answers a question, *corroborating* accounts, *contextualizing* accounts, and *sorting out* causal relationships.

Being able to engage these strategies fluently and automatically, or even with conscious effort, is the process by which first-order historical understandings are constructed. Therefore, the strategies and the concepts-in-use become indispensable. Gathering and interpreting data on where students are in their progression toward employing them successfully is crucial for history teachers who need to work out the depth of those students' sense making about the past (e.g., Truman's rationale for using the bomb). To repeat, historical-thinking capability is the *sine qua non* of historical understanding. Thus, being able to interpret task data on what a student can do with what she knows (thinking) becomes as important as, and perhaps even more important than, making sense of what she says she knows about the past (understanding). I simply cannot emphasize that point enough.

Historical Understanding

Making sense of the past results in the capability to tell a story or produce a narrative that carefully and cautiously explains, for example, how Truman thought and rationalized his reasoning as he elected to use the world's first nuclear weapon. It requires a consideration of the various ways the evidence about his reasoning stacks up. It also treats alternative interpretations on its way to presenting its argumentative thesis. It utilizes first-order concepts such as "the Communist threat," "allies and axis powers," "the Pacific and Western Fronts," and the like to support that thesis. Effectively, narrative argument puts on display an understanding that addresses the question of what Truman was thinking.

From these characteristics we can identify those aspects of understanding that we hope to see in the ways students respond to the question. On the one hand, and following aspects of the ELA Common Core Standards, we are looking for sound *argumentation*, cogent *communication*, attention to *supportive detail*, *persuasiveness*, and good grammatical and syntactical *structure*. But we are also interested, perhaps even more profoundly, in the historical substance of the narrative. How does it cite and deal with alternative and possibly *competing interpretations*? Does the narrative successfully employ *first-order concepts* to make its case? Does it remain within the confines of the *historical context* of the period, or pronounce *judgment* on Truman only from the vantage point of the present?

All these italicized features or characteristics of the narrative argument and the historical-thinking process can and, I would argue, need to become the focus of rubrics and coding schemes by which students are assessed. Applying them turns students' performance assessment data into evidence. From that evidence, we can diagnose where students are in their progressions and make evidence-based decisions about how to move them forward as necessary. The added value is that, by assessing and interpreting in this way, we also gain the potential to make claims about where students are with respect to reading and writing, as specified by the ELA Common Core Standards, even though the ELA remain entirely silent on what specific historical understandings students might develop.

Rubrics and Coding Schemes

Interpreting WMC Tasks

Evidence of Understanding. With the sorts of tasks that gauge historical understanding, the weighting structure becomes a type of coding scheme or rubric for turning the responses students generate into meaningful evidence. Since there are four options, theoretically all such weighted items should follow a similar option-weighting structure. To review, the best option—4 points in Beard's scheme— would be the most defensible and best evidence-supported choice given the prompt and the nature of students' learning experiences with the subject of that prompt. The 2-point option would be technically accurate, but less precise and evidence defensible than the best option. It could anticipate the reasoning of the best option but falls short of fully articulating it. The 1-point option is also technically acceptable, but again, is even less defensible because it appeals to a common, thinly reasoned, and perhaps stereotypical conception (e.g., once the Japanese saw the bomb's destructive force, Truman thought the war would end quickly). The 0-point option would be patently incorrect.

There could be almost any number of variations on the weighting theory used for items that assess understanding. The benefit of Beard's approach is that, first, it respects the interpretive nature of developing historical understandings, and second, it is designed to allow her to gather evidence of how her students reason. In short, it shows her how to identify where her students are in their progressions from weaker to stronger understanding. If her students are prone, for instance, to selecting 0- or 1-point options, she has much work to do in mov- ing them toward reasoning more carefully and deeply. If, on the other hand, she witnesses a large number of 2-point selections, she knows she is moving them along (assuming pre-assessment evidence showed less adequate responses), but has not fully succeeded in teaching them how to think their way through to the more sophisticated 4-point choice. She has diagnostic evidence in hand that can be turned into additional in-class learning opportunities.

As I noted in the last chapter, Beard makes her weighting structure and theoretical rationale transparent. When she returns the assessments to students, she takes time to open up space for students to examine their responses and talk about individual items. This gives Beard yet one more opportunity to hear where her students are in their think- ing as they work through options. Often, what students say is particu- larly revealing in ways that reinforce the evidence of understanding that the items produce. Occasionally, students succeed at making a case that their selection, say, of a 2-point option deserves consideration as a 4-point choice. Assessment, instead of being little more than a final judgment, functions as yet one more powerful learning opportunity. It moves learning from a testing-culture pivot toward an embrace of a learning culture.

Evidence of Thinking Practice. WMC tasks can also be marshaled to gather evidence of how students think about employing procedural concepts. As we saw in the last chapter, items can be written around concepts such as accounts, evidence, contextualization, causation, and progress/decline. Again, a theoretical structure for weighting is necessary if the goal is to yield evidence that possesses diagnostic power. Beard draws from the same theoretical weighting structure she applies with regard to items that measure historical understanding. She believes that keeping principles consistent helps students know what to expect and learn how to more carefully assess the assessment approach. In this sense, she argues that she is teaching them to become self-assessors.

In considering how students make sense of procedural concepts, the 4-point option articulates what she has been teaching students in class about how to employ them. The 2-point option anticipates its higher point predecessor but does not quite articulate the issue as clearly and can lack a certain key attribute. The 1-point option is, again, technically correct, but even more simplistic and can be attractive if a student's thinking about the issue is not well developed. For example, students without much experience learning to think historically often imagine that an account must contain eyewitness testimony in order to be considered primary and accurate. Although eyewitness testimony is considered a primary account, not all accounts that are considered primary contain eyewitness testimony, and not all eyewitness testimony is accurate. That's the rub. As before, the 0-point option is simply and rather blatantly incorrect given the prompt.

Any number of procedural concepts can be assessed using this weighting structure. The most imaginative items attempt to assess a procedural concept-in-use. That is, the item is written in a way that situates the concept within a context in which it could be employed (the prompt) and then asks the students to identify its best in-use option from among four possibilities. Here is another example, one different from those illustrated in Chapter 3 and designed to suggest the range of possibilities.

The **cause** of the Jamestown colony's "starving time" in the winter of 1609–1610 is not fully understood because

   a. We lack sufficient **evidence** to hypothesize accurately about the **cause.**

   b. The secondary **account evidence** contradicts primary **account** reports.

   c. The **evidence** presents a conflicting set of ideas about what occurred.

   d. Recent **evidence** indicates there was no period of starvation that winter.

In this example, the context is stated in the prompt, Jamestown colony's early "starving time." The concepts-in-use are bolded: causation, accounts-as-evidence, and evidence corroboration. The prompt and options trace a line of reasoning from accounts to evidence and then on to how that evidence might be corroborated in order for investigators to make causal claims. Of course, this item is useful and valid only if learners have an opportunity to investigate the "starving time" in the winter of 1609–1610.

Option (d) is the 0-point choice here because there is some reasonably clear evidence that starvation did beset the British colonists in Jamestown during that fateful winter. Option (b) receives 1 point because, although there are some contradictory accounts, we can still do some conjecturing about causes, but with caution. Option (c) simply states the idea embedded in option (b) more clearly and concisely and therefore it receives 2 points. The 4-point option is (a) because a definitive claim about cause is beyond the investigator's reach given the mixed evidence at hand. In keeping with the weighting theory, option (b) is a common choice among more novice historical investigators. They often think that when accounts offer up conflicting evidence nothing further can be said because they have yet to learn the finer points of how investigators, by using rhetorical hedges and presenting causation from different angles, can still make claims that illuminate without necessarily providing full closure.[4]

In order to demonstrate solid thinking on this type of WMC item, learners need to be able to reason about how the concepts in question are used during the procedures designed to address a question—in this case, what caused the Jamestown "starving time." The item helps teachers see the ways in which learners are doing that thinking and at what level. That the item principally treats key procedural concepts allows for the subject matter context of the prompt to be modified in ways that permit its repeated use across a set of topics or units. As long as a topic attempts to link causal claims with evidentiary support, roughly the same types of options can reappear with modified prompts. The scoring structure (rubric) and rationale also remain, giving teachers long-range, longitudinal evidence of how their students are thinking about these concepts-in-use and whether they are making progress.

Remember that it is deeply important to keep track of where students are in the ways they think about and use such concepts. How students wield them as they address historical questions will either facilitate or retard their understandings.

Interpreting Written-response Tasks

As we saw, these types of tasks can take many different forms depending upon what a teacher wishes to assess. Because the more common written task frequently involves some variation on a document-based question, let's begin there.

Document-Based Questions.   Clearly a rubric must be developed for and applied to these DBQ responses. If Beard uses such assessment items, the question she must answer is what, exactly, the rubric should assess. How that question is answered depends on (a) the target goals of the thinking and understanding to be assessed and (b) the nature of the prompt and its historical context. These two criteria work in concert with and shape each other.

Characteristic	Score of 8–9 (highest possible)
Thesis	Clear, well developed thesis.
Understanding of the question	Understands complexity of the question; deals with all parts of the question in depth.
Analysis	Provides effective analysis of the question; some imbalance permissible.
Documentary evidence	Effectively uses a substantial number of documents. Documents supplement analysis and are balanced with outside information.
Supportive information	Supports thesis with substantial, relevant information. Outside information is balanced with use of documents in the analysis of the question.
Grammar and structure	May contain insignificant errors.
Organization and writing style	Well organized and well written.

(Available online at http://shs.westport.k12.ct.us/jdamico/APUS/Rubrics.htm)

FIGURE 4.1. Document-Based Question Rubric (Westport Public Schools).

With DBQ items, it has been common to tilt the assessment rubrics toward writing strategies. Consider this example from Westport, Connecticut, public schools. Notice the emphasis on writing capabilities in the scoring rubric categories as well as in the description of what would constitute the highest score. One could make an argument that only two of the seven scoring categories—Documentary Evidence and Analysis—are clearly specific to history questions, if we take the learning model described in Chapter 2 seriously. The other five (of seven) categories pertain more to general writing strategies (developing a thesis; making sense of a question; drawing from background, supportive ideas; grammar and structure; writing style) that could be relevant to any domain question asked that would draw from documents. In this sense they are quite generic.

The rubric scoring categories from Westport schools no doubt draw from the published guidelines established by the College Board, the organization that runs the Advanced Placement program and typically includes DBQs on the exams it administers. Here are its guidelines for

For an 8–9 Score Essay (highest two possibilities):

- Contains a clear, well-developed **thesis** that addresses all parts of the question:
- Presents an effective **analysis** of the topic; treatment of multiple parts may be somewhat uneven:
- Effectively uses a substantial number of **documents**.
- Develops the thesis with substantial and relevant **outside information**.
- May contain **minor errors** that do not detract from the quality of the essay.

(Available at http://apcentral.collegeboard.com/apc/public/repository/ap12_us_history_scoring_guidelines.pdf)

FIGURE 4.2. College Board Scoring Guidelines for Document-Based Questions in U.S. History.

comparative purposes. The commonalities with the Westport scoring characteristics are highlighted.

It is not hard to see again the rather generic nature of the scoring guidelines. The second and third bullets (of five) potentially represent the only history-specific categories. What constitutes an "effective analysis" (the second bullet) is not specified. However, the category does point toward using procedural concepts and cognitive strategies without saying so. Using a "substantial number of documents" suggests a technical counting approach to interpreting the responses, without indicating to what end the documents might be used. Presumably it involves producing a thesis and an engaging in an "effective analysis." Yet none of this is made clear via an appeal to a robust, history-specific learning model. As a result, the outcome is likely to be of limited use to classroom teachers or their students.

My point here is that we can draw from the learning model to design more robust rubrics that help us better make sense of what students are thinking and thus understanding about the past. Applying the learning model to an accounts-based question that Beard had asked—What was Truman thinking when he choose to use the atomic bomb against Japan in 1945?—we would expect students at their best to display a number of different cognitive capabilities in writing. These would include, but not necessarily be limited to, (1) clearly *establishing and arguing an interpretive position* (i.e., a thesis), based on the range of possibilities, for example, that Beard considered in class; (2) *citing evidence* from the accounts provided to defend that position; (3) *corroborating that evidence* across accounts (i.e., intertextually); while (4) *assessing the status* of those accounts as evidence (i.e., establishing account reliability, thus arguing against "less reliable" accounts as satisfactory evidence); and (5) arguing the position within the *historical context* of the period.[5]

In effect, we have five rubric categories here: (1) Establishes/Argues Position, (2) Citing Evidence, (3) Corroboration, (4) Assessing Account Status, and (5) Contextualization.[6] As with the weighting theory used in WMC items, we need to scale a range of possible ways of performing on each category, from nonexistent to superlative. Points can be awarded by category for each type of performance. To illustrate, Beard's rubric looks like this:

Applying this sort of detailed rubric to students' essays would yield detailed evidence of the capacity to work with the concepts and strategies described by the learning model. The first category, *Establishes/Argues Position*, also demands a performance that should enable an interpretation of students' historical understandings. Yet we must keep in mind that it is difficult to say with exact precision what was on Truman's mind in July of 1945. There is no full or even partial record that we know of for each of his thoughts during the moments in which he made his decision. He does offer some thoughts after the fact. But even then we cannot be quite sure how they were shaped by ensuing events and experiences. Memory can be an odd creature.

Nevertheless, there are a number of intriguing interpretations of Truman's decision that could be argued individually or in combinations. Beard considered many of them in class. What she hopes for hinges on witnessing students who can draw from one or more of these interpretations and make a compelling, explanatory case. Seeing those exemplars is what she means by historical understanding. And she has a rubric category at the ready to interpret and assess them.

Although it does not use the language of multiple causation in considering different interpretations of Truman's thoughts, the first rubric category works with this procedural concept implicitly. In that sense, teachers can infer the ways in which students apply this concept as they

Establishes/Argues Position

4 Clearly stakes out a position on what was thought (or occurred), argues convincingly, refutes other possible interpretations

3 Stakes out position—argument not as clear, concise, direct or as strong as 4, weaker refutation of other interpretations

2 Takes a position, supported, but questionable argument, no refutation of other positions despite use of conditional language

1 Takes a position but does little to effectively argue that position, may use some conditional language

0 Takes no position, avoids interpretation, argues that making one is too difficult and thus does not address the prompt

Citing Evidence

4 Refers directly to specific accounts (more than one); mentions by name (e.g., title, doc. 1, author)

3 Refers to accounts; does not cite consistently by name or frequency (as in a 4)

2 Generally alludes to evidence, but draws from only one account; ignores accounts not aligned to interpretation

1 No mention of evidence despite offering an interpretation

0 No mention of evidence as though accounts were not read/did not exist

Corroboration

4 Compares/contrasts multiple accounts/perspectives directly to form interpretation

3 Compares/contrasts accounts to form interpretation but not as consistently, clearly, or directly as a 4

2 Allusions (indirect) to comparing/contrasting perspectives, but ignores some accounts or perspectives

1 No evidence of corroboration because of unidirectional, simplistic interpretation

0 No evidence of corroboration as though multiple perspectives in accounts did not exist/not possible

Assessing Account Status

4 Direct presence of evaluations of specific sources' quality/reliability in forming interpretation

3 Occasional evaluations of sources' quality/reliability, but not as direct or consistent as a 4

2 Evaluates only that/those source/s used in singular interpretation

1 Non existent evaluations; singular, unidirectional interpretation

0 No evaluations, as though none were necessary because establishing a thesis and conducting an interpretation is considered impossible or too difficult

Continued overleaf

Contextualization

4 Stays within historical context and makes comments that reflect self-awareness of doing so; no presentism

3 Stays within historical context, no presentism

2 Argument analyses/mixes both past and presentist perspectives

1 Solely presentist as though decision event happened yesterday and contemporaneous normative standards apply

0 No bounding within historical context because establishing context was not seen as necessary

FIGURE 4.3. Assessment Scoring Rubric for Interpreting an Accounts-Based Question on Truman's Atomic-Bomb Decision.

lay out their explanatory cases. For example, the rubric includes references to dealing with multiple interpretations. These interpretations effectively represent arguments about various circumstances surrounding, or understandings of, the late-war terrain that caused Truman to choose as he did. They are "causes" of his thinking (e.g., he sought to use the bomb to end the war quickly, thus avoiding massive casualties associated with a ground invasion). With some language tweaking, the rubric category could be modified to deal more explicitly with the concept of multiple causation. Understanding causation is crucial to understanding the past.

If cogently nuanced historical understanding of Truman's decision is what Beard is after, why not then simplify the rubric by dropping the other four categories? Why does the rubric need to appear so complex and multifaceted? These are good questions. The most straightforward response in defense of Beard's rubric is the proposition that, adhering closely to the learning model, there is little historical understanding without historical thinking. Therefore, in order to arrive at an evidence-defensible argument about Truman's reasons for choosing to use the bomb, students must be able to read and analyze the accounts provided; assess their status (reliability); convert them into evidence for making claims, which involves corroboration; and argue them within the context of the historical period.

These mental practices, among others earlier described, combine to allow for a written performance of an understanding. If they are necessary, then they need to be assessed and interpreted. That in turn enables history teachers to see more fully how students construct their understanding. Put a different way, the learning model predicts that a written understanding that appears weak is likely the consequence of a breakdown in one or more aspects of the thinking process. The rubric's other four categories can help identify where that breakdown occurs. With evidence in hand, its diagnostic power permits teachers to work with individual students on their particular cognitive difficulties. This assistive goal is to improve the likelihood that understanding will deepen for those students as their thinking processes become more competent. All five rubric categories work in concert to achieve this end. The sharper and more complete they are, the more diagnostic power they hold.

Single-Account Interpretive Essays (SAIEs). With SAIEs, Beard is trying to (1) get purchase on the process by which students interpret an account (or cartoon, photograph, painting) and then to (2) assess what sense students make of it. Since the well-honed process of interpretation would include attention to *identifying* what the account was, *attributing it* to an author, *assessing the perspective* of its author (writer, painter, cartoonist, photographer), and *contextualizing* it, these form her rubric categories. Beard borrows the contextualization category from the preceding DBQ-style question rubric and modifies it slightly to fit her SAIE prompt. The interpretation rubric looks like this.

The SAIE example from Beard's assessment work that I provided in Chapter 3 turned on students reading of "Truman's Reflection on the Atomic Bombings" (penned in 1953). So, for the second part of the prompt, students are asked to make sense of what Truman is saying about his reasons for choosing to use the bomb on Japan and explain why they think as they do. Beard uses a modified version of the *Establishes/Argues Position* category from the preceding DBQ-style question rubric.

An alternative assessment strategy for this type of SAIE task, as we saw in the last chapter, involved posing different questions, such as (1) In what particular ways does this account shed light on Truman's decision?, (2) Is this account reliable for understanding Truman's reasons and why or why not?, and (3) How did you go about interpreting this account? These questions prompt students to engage in similar thinking process and writing about their understandings as the preceding

Identifying the Account

3 Clearly and correctly identifies the account, dates it, and speaks to its origins

2 Correctly identifies the account, adds date, but does not note origin

1 Only correctly states account's identification by name

0 Does not identify the account or provides a mistaken identity

Attributing the Account to an Author

3 Attributes account to correct author and speaks to who the author is

2 Only notes correct author

1 Notes incorrect author

0 Does not attribute the account

Assessing Author Perspective

3 Clearly describes the author's perspective using context-embedded cues from the text (or painting, photo, etc.) itself

2 Describes author perspective, but without noting any context cues

1 Notes a perspective but misses details and/or appears to mis-interpret author

0 Neglects to assess the author's perspective

Contextualizing the Account

3 Explains author perspective within historical context and makes comments that reflect self-awareness of doing so; no presentism

2 Analyzes author perspective mixing both past and presentist perspectives

1 Solely presentist judgments of author's perspective as though only contemporaneous normative standards apply

0 No bounding within historical context because author is considered too difficult to understand

FIGURE 4.4. Beard's SAIE Part-One Rubric.

Establishes/ Argues Position

4 Clearly stakes out a position on what Truman says he thought/reasoned, argues convincingly citing account-embedded context cues/details

3 Stakes out position—argument not as clear, concise, direct or as strong as 4, weaker use of account context cues/details

2 Takes a position, supported but questionable argument/explanation of what Truman says he was thinking, missed details from account

1 Takes a position but does little to effectively argue that position, no support with actual account context cues/details

0 Takes no position, no interpretation, or argues that making one is too difficult, or does not address the prompt

FIGURE 4.5. Beard's SAIE Part-Two Rubric.

SAIE and DBQ-style tasks. Similar rubrics, therefore, could be applied here (see Figures 4.3 and 4.5). However, a different interpretation strategy could be employed to turn responses to the third question into data that represented students' use of cognitive strategies.

A combination of those strategies could be listed in a box in the left margin with the Truman text at the center. In the right margin, spaces could be provided in which students could identify which strategies they thought they were using as they read the text. The version Beard uses looks like this.

By observing the types of strategies students select, the frequencies with which they select those strategies, and at what point in the text they choose those strategies as they read, Beard obtains a rough profile of how students are working with them. Together with other rubrics that interpret evidence of cognitive strategy use, this second approach adds multiple data points that offer opportunities to corroborate and substantiate claims about how students are thinking historically.[7]

Strategies that you might use while reading and analyzing the text:	The account to be interpreted: "Truman's Reflections on the Atomic Bombings" (1953)	Strategies you were using as you read and analyzed. Put the code number of the strategy at the left in the spaces provided as you read and analyze.
Code # and Description: 1. Identifying the account 2. Attributing it to an author 3. Assessing the author's perspective 4. Judging how reliable the author's account is 5. Reading closely for key details 6. Looking for evidence of the author's claims 7. Reading account in context	THE WHITE HOUSE Washington January 12, 1953 My Dear Professor Cate; Your letter of December 6, 1952 has just been delivered to me. When the message came to Potsdam that a successful atomic explosion had taken place in New Mexico . . . . (and so on to the end of the excerpt)	_____ _____ _____ _____ _____ _____ _____ _____ _____ _____ _____

FIGURE 4.6. Beard's Alternative SAIE Rubric.

Project Presentations. Webpage designs and multimedia presentation tasks also require students to put on display how they think and understand. Combinations of any of the aforementioned interpretive rubrics could be applied to such products. Typically such rubrics, if they have been used at all, have focused more on the historical understandings students construct (e.g., Truman's reason[s] for choosing to drop the atomic bomb) and considerably less on the thinking processes they engaged in order to arrive at those understandings. As I have been arguing, this significantly limits the range of evidence teachers can obtain about their students' growing and changing learning capabilities. I am encouraging the application of interpretive rubrics that are relevant to *both* thinking processes and subsequent understandings, not one or the other. They are inextricably interconnected in history education. And they can be applied to project presentations as readily as to DBQ-type essays or SAIEs.

Interpreting Beliefs About History

What students believe history is, how they see it is as distinct or not from the past, and how they go about providing warrants for the claims they make about historical events turn out to be crucial to their ability to move forward in the ways they make sense of history. The challenge for learners in history is to adjust their beliefs in such a way that they can successfully coordinate their roles as knowers of the past with the demands of understanding what can be known, or said to be known. This is not as easy as it sounds, and the learning model makes that quite clear.

Initially, learners develop the idea that the past and history are one and the same. In effect, this is a belief in a concrete, knowable past that speaks itself clearly. Learners appear to be saying that history is what happened, as simple as that. It is as if history is like a chronicle, unfolding minute by minute and action by action the way the present appears to unfold. The knower, and a passive one at that, has very little role other than to see how that past has therefore unfolded itself chronologically. When these learners encounter situations in which there are gaps in what can be known because no one kept records or accounts of occurrences, or because what records may have been kept were lost, they are pressed into an interpretive process. Now, as active knowers, they need to fill in the missing pieces in order for the past to become known.

With this realization, another problem quickly arises. How far can the active knower go in making those interpretations? Can the knower fill in the missing pieces, so to speak, in whatever way he or she wishes? Is it an interpretive free-for-all, one in which doing history becomes little more than a vulgar subjective act? Learners often swing rapidly from a passive role to what we might call an overactive role, over-interpreting the residue of the past that's left behind and filling in gaps willy-nilly with their opinions. Neither the passive nor overactive roles are particularly helpful in coming to understand the past. In fact, both arrest understanding.

Seasoned investigators who participate in communities of inquirers realize that, once the knower recognizes the need for an active role, and in order to avoid a type of careless interpretive subjectivity that can follow, rules need to govern the process. We might call these rules interpretive criteria. That is, to make a defensible claim about what the past means—to do history as it were—involves adhering to those criteria. One of the most crucial criteria in the study of history is the capacity to draw on convincing, preponderant evidence to defend a set of claims and be honest about when that evidence is thin or non-existent.[8] Doing so is what I mean when I say that the passive knower needs to become active, but then to coordinate his or her belief system around a criteria-referenced structure that attempts to place some reasonable limits on the reach of that activity. The community of historical investigators, of which young learners can be a part, debates, attempts to agree on, and then operates from what those criteria are, while also being open to revisiting them again as necessary.

Working with and adhering to such criteria, and the ways in which they help coordinate the role of knower with respect to what can to be known (or said to be known), constitutes a belief system that allows historical practice to be undertaken. Without it, historical thinking practices bang into all manner of impasses that block understanding. Beard attempts to move her students' beliefs toward this criteria-infused stance. To check on her progress she draws from a short beliefs questionnaire. As we saw in the last chapter, she uses a set of statements that express beliefs, often four each that represent the passive-knower position, the overactive-knower position, and the criteria-structured position. Here is an example of the statements she uses.

Passive-Knower Belief Statements

1. There is no difference between the past and history.
2. Historical facts speak for themselves.
3. History is what happened in the past.
4. It is impossible to know anything about the past because none of us were there.

Overactive-Knower Belief Statements

1. The past is simply what the investigator makes it to be.
2. Historical investigators know that history is just a matter of opinion.
3. Since we cannot really know what happened in the past, we can believe whatever we want to about it.
4. Historical claims cannot be justified since they are simply a matter of interpretation.

Criteria-Structured Belief Statements[9]

1. Comparing sources and understanding author perspective are crucial components of the process of investigating the past.
2. History is a critical inquiry into the past.
3. Reasonable interpretations of the past can be constructed even in the presence of conflicting evidence.
4. History is the reasonable reconstruction of past occurrences based on the available evidence.

Beard randomly distributes the statements across the 12-item questionnaire. Students are asked to strongly agree, agree, disagree, or strongly disagree with each statement by circling its representative number to the right of the statements (see the example in Chapter 3). If this questionnaire's observational results are to be diagnostically meaningful, the question Beard must answer relates to what she can make of how her students respond.

Beard would consider her pedagogical and curricular efforts a success if her students would consistently *disagree/strongly disagree* with all the passive-knower and overactive-knower statements, and *agree/ strongly agree* with all the criteria-structured statements. This rarely happens, but it is one of her goals nonetheless. What Beard typically sees instead is a lot of inconsistency: agreements with some passive- and overactive-knower statements and disagreements with some criteria-structured statements.

Establishing a measure of *consistency* is the rubric Beard uses to interpret the results of this questionnaire.[10] There are 12 statements, 4 in each category. Beard looks at the responses her students select and counts each time a student disagrees/strongly disagrees with a passive- or overactive-knower statement and agrees/strongly agrees with a criteria-structured statement. For example, if student Jennifer disagrees with 6 of the 8 passive- and overactive-knower statements and agrees with 3 of the criteria-structured statements, Beard expresses this as a ratio, or 9 of 12 possibilities. Therefore, Jennifer obtains a *consistency score* of 75%. To claim success in moving Jennifer to a criteria-structured belief position (or stance), Beard sets the bar high—90% or higher, at least a score of 11 of the 12.

Beard typically administers the beliefs questionnaire three times in a semester course—beginning, middle, and near the end. She tells her students that (a) there are no right or wrong responses, (b) it is not an evaluated exercise, (c) she uses the results to better understand their thinking, and (d) all she wishes is for them to respond to each statement as honestly as possible. Beards believes that her students, generally speaking, understand and respond accordingly. The results prove powerfully useful in helping Beard see if the exercises she relies on, such as the "What Was Truman Thinking?" lesson, help her students move toward the criterialist position and away from the other two, and if students are not moving in this direction, how she can redouble her efforts to stress the important criteria structure upon which sound historical work is based.

Informal, In-class Assessment Interpretations

Many of the aforementioned rubric categories also can be used to informally assess classroom-based exercises. They can be applied individually or in clusters, depending upon the focus of a lesson or lesson sequence. Running records of the way in which students *cite evidence* and/or *contextualize* their interpretations during a discussion of a series of accounts, for example, could be readily employed via a type of checklist. This might be valuable in tracking the learning progressions of particular students who struggle with constructively applying these criteria. Doing so over time gives purchase on whether or not more individual attention needs to be offered to those students in order to enhance their progress.

Communicating Interpretive Outcomes

As I noted, Beard makes a habit of taking time to be as transparent as possible about the weighting rationales she uses on the WMC items, as well as the content of her other rubrics. She holds open discussions when she returns assessments in order to show students how her assessment practices work and what interpretations she draws from them about how students are performing. Students can also debate her interpretive rationales and even the categories themselves. She does the same with student results on essays, single-account interpretations, and project presentations.

Her goal is to communicate clearly her expectations and the criteria she applies to measure her success at reaching those expectations. She wants her students to grow to be as good at self-assessment as they are at meeting her expectations. She also keeps the process open to adjustments, even ones suggested and rationalized by her students. Finally, as often as she can, she reminds her charges that what she does, how she assesses, is as much a process of gauging student progression in learning to think historically and understand the past as it is a yardstick that measures the quality of her teaching practices.

How does Beard translate assessment outcomes into letter grades, that ubiquitous practice of communicating something about relative achievement? This is a tricky question. Grades by definition involve layering or stratifying. Traditionally, grades have operated in concert with a sorting and selecting function in which schooling engages. That is, they have been employed to separate excellent student achievement from all its lesser variations. Beard's assessment approach is much more about diagnosing student learning difficulties in ways that permit her to attempt to reverse them than it is about a sorting, selecting, and stratifying tactic. The latter fits more neatly within what we might call a testing/accountability culture. Beard's approach, we could say, aligns better with the values of a learning culture. The two could not be more different in attitude and orientation. Yet in Beard's school system, they still rely on traditional letter grading as a means of communication about achievement (or something).

This means that Beard must engage in the difficult task of translating the results of her assessments into some type of letter grade. Because her desire is to communicate about progression in learning to think and understand, she rarely relies on the low end of the letter grading scale unless a student simply refuses to attempt what she asks. Beard frequently pre-assesses, meaning that she obtains multiple, similar observations of student thinking and understanding. This gives her a baseline, or a series of baselines, from which she can gauge progressions (or the lack thereof). In turn, this means letter grades such as B and C become two different markers or levels of *emerging* progress, and the letter A becomes an indicator of *accomplishment* relative to her criteria. She makes this idea clear to her students. To illustrate, here is an example of what she does with the weighted items she uses.

If Beard consistently draws upon her option-structure rationale, on an assessment of 10 such weighted items with 4 points being the maximum score for each item, a 40-point total rather obviously would represent *accomplished*, or a letter grade of A. One way Beard thinks about what remains of the possible point totals is linked to her item-rationale theory. Put simply, a total score of 20 on this same 10-item assessment indicates that a student who attains this score has repeatedly selected defensible but somewhat more limited options given the array of choices. A total score of 10 represents a student who is consistently selecting a technically acceptable but perhaps weak and/or stereotypical set of options that reflect less disciplined thinking and understanding. A total score of 0 is self-defining; it is something Beard very rarely witnesses.

Understood this way, we can see general ranges of outcomes that indicate where students might be in their progressions. For instance, scores at or beyond 30 points (but not yet 40 points) on this 10-item assessment suggest that students scoring in that range are getting close to approaching the category of *accomplished*. In other words, the majority of the time, those students are selecting 4-point options, but the occasional lesser-point choice selected. So, such students show *strong emergent* progress. Beard awards such scores within the letter grade range of B, while reminding her students regularly what this means in the way I just described it.

Beard describes students who score in a range from 10 to 29 on such an assessment as *moderate emergent* progression. They receive a letter grade within the range of C. Those who score below 10 points, something quite rare in Beard's experience, are considered *weak emergent* and receive a letter grade in the range of D, again with the commensurate explanation. Beard employs a similar approach to converting written assessment exercises and project presentation outcomes into letter grades, while adjusting the score ranges for the number of rubric categories she applies and the range and nature of possible scores within each category (e.g., Figure 4.3). Baseline scores against which subsequent scores can be measured are also crucial for making final determinations about how to judge emergent progress categories.

Because of her deep commitment to learning progression, Beard offers a variety of opportunities for students to improve their assessment-score outcomes, even some after the fact (e.g., rewriting essay questions). The result typically helps students improve, particularly because of the transparency of her interpretive rubrics. Beard also finds that such an approach does more to encourage students to improve the quality of their work than a sole reliance on letter grades untethered to clear learning progressions might. This, she believes, is how assessment should operate in a culture that values learning for all students, rather than one that prioritizes sorting, stratifying, and selecting out the best.

Getting parents to understand what she does is a greater challenge for Beard. Parents have been deeply socialized and seduced by the testing/accountability culture vocabulary and its sorting, selecting, and stratifying approach. The vocabulary of the learning culture (e.g., diagnosis, learning progression, evidence-based pedagogical judgment, remediation) is not foreign to parents, but it often carries less currency for them despite its promise. To explain her approach, Beard frequently augments her grading scale with concrete examples of student work—that is, evidence of their progressions or lack thereof within specific assessment contexts—in order to help them make sense of her approach and criteria. In the end, parents usually comprehend that Beard is using assessment to serve a culture of learning, rather than as a sorting, selecting, and stratifying system. Many come to recognize and appreciate the value of Beard's approach for *their* children.

Notes

1 Pellegrino, et al., *Knowing What Students Know.*
2 Some researchers have attempted to "see" learning take place, for example, by tracking changes in brain activity through magnetic resonance imaging (MRI) or by charting changes in the brain's electrical activity via attached electrodes. Such efforts still require interpretation strategies for making sense of those changes. Those strategies require some sort of a theoretical model for explaining what shifts in brain pattern activity mean. Metaphorically, MRI data, for instance, are a like assessment task data in that they need to be interpreted with respect to a change model. In that sense, inferencing is still in play and "learning remains invisible" despite efforts to actually observe it.
3 Here again, I am using the term *author* very broadly to include the creator of a painting, a pottery shard, a photograph, a cartoon, a YouTube clip, and so on.
4 For more on this, see, for example, Lee and Shemilt, "A Scaffold Not a Cage: Progression and Progression Models in History," *Teaching History, 113* (2003), pp. 13–23.
5 A rubric category for contextualization is particularly important in this case because it is relatively easy to scan images of the bombs' destructive powers, especially with regard to Japanese civilians; imagine the long-term consequences; and level a scathing moral indictment of Truman. It can be done without ever coming to understand the brutal scale of the war and the moral atrocities perpetrated by all sides on civilian populations. This does not necessarily make the act morally impugnable. But

contextualization is an act of understanding—in this case, of the moral am-
biguities inherent in the decision facing Truman. Beard wants her students
to achieve that sort of understanding.

6 Since Truman's decision and the unleashing of atomic weaponry so radically
changed the world from August 1945 onward, a sixth rubric category could
be added that treats *historical significance*. That is, applying such a scaled rubric
category would allow for assessing students' understanding of the significance
of the decision and its world-changing dynamics. It is also possible to apply
any additional rubric category without actually making it visible to students.
In other words, if Beard chooses the addition, she could adopt it strictly for
her own diagnostic purposes: It would give her evidence of her students'
capability to employ a second-order concept (historical significance) without
specific prompting by the task. Students would, therefore, not be held ac-
countable for failing to do so. But Beard could use the outcome to obtain
evidence of the unprompted students' capabilities nonetheless.

7 Many of the rubric categories described in Figures 4.3 to 4.6 could be
applied to interpret verbal-report protocols and video-recorded lessons,
if those observational methods were chosen to gather evidence of student
thinking and understanding.

8 For more on this point, see Allan Megill, *Historical Knowledge, Historical
Error: A Contemporary Guide to Practice* (Chicago: University of Chicago
Press, 2007).

9 We might call the passive knower a naïve objectivist, since he defers to the
power of the object, as though the past was like, say, an automobile, something any sentient person could easily identify because the object tells us
(or appears to at least) what it is without any fuss. The overactive knower
might be termed a naive subjectivist because of her penchant for thinking
that unsubstantiated opinion is sufficient. The criteria-structured knower
might simply be called a criterialist. One must systematically learn about
the criteria and how to wield them from a more knowledgeable other (e.g.,
Beard). Success at that learning process, therefore, erases the applicability of
the modifying term *naïve*.

10 The research work on epistemic beliefs in history indicates that expert
historical investigators (e.g., historians) are routinely consistent in their
agreements with criteria-structured belief statements and their disagreements with the other two sets of statements. See Liliana Maggioni, Bruce
VanSledright, and Patricia Alexander, "Walking on the Borders: A Measure of Epistemic Cognition in History, *Journal of Experimental Education,*
77 (2009), pp. 187–213.

5

STANDARDS, ASSESSMENTS, TESTING, AND QUESTIONS OF ALIGNMENT

The kinds of assessment tasks and interpretation structures I have been advocating in the preceding chapters are clearly more complex to design and possibly even to administer than traditional items. You might be asking, Why go to the trouble? Addressing this question appeals to a range of arguments, some of which I've already sketched—the sharp limits of traditional testing approaches, for example. Other types of arguments underpin the ELA Common Core Standards as well as the social studies inquiry framework. Similar arguments also emanate from a number of organizations (e.g., Achieve and the Smarter Balanced Assessment Consortium, or SBAC) and assessment scholars.[1]

Many of these arguments boil down to two interconnected claims. The first maintains that our common teaching-learning-testing strategies are rooted in outdated assumptions about how children and adolescents learn. As a result, our learning targets, curricula, and earlier standards, as well as the testing assumptions built into such policies as *No Child Left Behind*, are no longer applicable in the 21st century. A second argument asserts that, in a fully globalized and digitized world, new types of career and employment demands make change necessary if the United States wishes to remain at the forefront of the world economy. Creativity, problem-solving capability, and the capacity to carefully analyze data and use those data to arrive at evidence-supported interpretations that can be employed to solve problems, rather than knowledge acquisition and retention for their own sake, becomes the new order of the day and the new expectation for career success. It's not so much what you know as it is what you can do with what you know.[2]

Take the Council of Chief State School Officers (CCSSO) as one example of an organization that is attempting to drive changes in how we think about teaching and learning, and especially assessing. In its EdSteps Framework (www.edsteps.org), CCSSO identifies five skills that its members believe are crucial to college, career, and life-readiness in the current century. These include writing, global competence, creativity, analyzing information, and problem solving. The organization points out that these five skills are not the only skills that are important, but this is where it wishes to begin if "achieving teaching and learning that prepares every child with the knowledge, skills, and competencies needed for lifelong learning, satisfying work, and citizenship" is the goal.[3]

The EdSteps Framework outlines the role of the United States in a global, competitive economy; describes the challenge of the achievement gap; and discusses the need for higher quality K-12 education if the United States is to retain a dominant place in that global economy. To help attain this goal, the EdSteps effort proposes three outcomes it wishes to achieve through its website portal: (1) provide access to a variety of forms of student schoolwork with highlighted examples of college and career readiness and signals of progression from novice to more competent, (2) produce exemplary tools that allow teachers to consistently identify and assess those college and career readiness markers, and (3) support students to accept ownership for their own learning. The Framework and its goals, CCSSO maintains, are closely linked to the ELA (and Mathematics) Common Core Standards.

For their part, the Common Core Standards for English/Language Arts and Mathematics make similar arguments. Goals such as college and career readiness for a globalized world, with its problem solving-based and skills-driven economy, factor heavily into the rhetoric of the

Common Core. The social studies inquiry framework also borrows the same type of language, even in so far as to include college, careers, and citizenship in part of its larger title.[4]

As such standards and frameworks documents typically go, indicators of what students are to be able to do populate the pages that follow arguments about college, career, and citizenship readiness. If we continue to focus on the ELA Common Core and the emerging social studies inquiry framework, we see far less a focus on what I am calling first-order types of knowledge students should know (aka content) and much more on strategies and thinking practices. These include indicators that reflect, for instance, EdSteps' (and other organizations') focus on analyzing information and problem solving, and the more complex forms of reading and writing that support such practices.

This all means that, should these standards and frameworks be adopted widely, teachers will very likely need to much more overtly emphasize the strategies and cognitive processes necessary to attain deeper first-order (content) understandings. In other words, the standards push the same idea I have been pressing, that understanding depends on being able to think, read, write, and analyze. Deep understanding is not something that happens in the absence of cognitive capabilities; it is a consequence of them.

This is a relatively profound shift in how educational goals are conceptualized. And, as the rhetoric of these organizations suggests, there is something of chorus building. If the reconceptualized goals are pursued with the fervency of that growing chorus, assessment practices will need to change along with them. Of course, that change remains to be seen, and it certainly is not a foregone conclusion.[5] However, it does bear close attention.

Looking ahead and planning for such change seems like a good idea, and I have been emphasizing that point. I think it fair to assume that in relatively short order, assessments that emerge from groups such as the Smarter Balanced Assessment Consortium will align in some form or another with those reordered educational goals. Taking the time to consider and construct different approaches to assessment, therefore, may well be more than worth the trouble, not to mention the fact that, if the rhetoric of the arguments turn out to be the right educational direction for the foreseeable future, and practices shift accordingly, assessment practices will have to follow. Finally, I'm also leaving aside perhaps the most important reason I described in the opening chapter: If we hope to see learning and understanding improve and deepen, an embrace of diagnostic assessment practices is likely the best direction that could be offered to teachers and students.[6]

Although designing and using such performative assessments may be worth the trouble, a number of other questions remain that are related to issues of alignment, testing/accountability regimes, and cost. I would like to spend the remainder of this final chapter taking a brief look at those questions. In doing so, I hope to suggest additional arguments about what still needs to happen with regard to the relationship between new standards and frameworks, reoriented teaching practices, and more valuable assessments if all the trouble taken to broker changes will be worth it.

Aligning New Assessments to What Exactly?

Answering this question may seem initially self-evident. Study the indicators identified, say, in the ELA Common Core and the social studies inquiry framework and write assessment items to measure the presence or absence of the actions defined by the indicator. So far, so good, right? Well, it depends. What is the source of those indicators? Where do they come from? Are they derived from a model of learning? And is the model domain/discipline specific?

In a recent article, a former history teacher turned history education researcher observed that when she was teaching history, she spent much time assigning, cultivating, and stressing good historical writing. As a result her students learned to write well. But she was always somewhat disappointed. Her students, who were good writers, often did very well in her class. But they performed well "even if their understanding of history, and the nature of historical argument, was average."[7] She attributes the problem here to the rubrics she was using.

If we revisit the assessment triangle once more to get some additional grasp on the nature of this rubrics problem, we see that rubrics are interpretive theories that we can apply to assessment task results (observations). In a sense, standards indicators almost directly identify rubrics, or at the very least they suggest what those rubrics might be. Indicators also imply tasks. We saw an example of this in Chapter 1, where I broke down three ELA Common Core indicators and suggested how they pointed toward tasks and rubrics. The missing piece in those standards documents was a description of the learning model from which the indicators were derived. If Pellegrino and colleagues are right, the learning model—if it is carefully theorized, underpinned by empirical research, and tied to learning progressions—frames the learning targets (indicators); the pedagogical approach, learning, and assessment activities (tasks); and the interpretive parameters of the assessment evidence (rubrics).[8] In the foregoing example from our former history teacher, apparently the problem hinged on a rubric that was misaligned to understanding history and the nature of good historical arguments. So to what was her rubric aligned?

As our history teacher-researcher points out, she was drawing from interpretive schemes that privileged generically defined good writing over good history-specific writing. During the past several decades, educational researchers have pointed out repeatedly that the subject actually matters.[9] Writing in science, writing in language arts, and writing in history share some features in common, but they also diverge in important ways. To teach students to write strong science essays, for example, differs from teaching them to write strong history essays. The generic tools necessary for good writing take one only so far. Then the specificity and goals of the subject matter domain take over. The same is true for reading. To do science and to do history, of which good reading and writing are both a part, turn out to be quite different enterprises.

What I am driving at here, as is our history teacher-researcher in her article, is that the learning model for teaching good writing (and reading) *in general* differs from the learning model for teaching good writing (and reading) *in history*. But because we have seemed reluctant to carefully and clearly articulate and then detail learning models, we appear to have assumed that an implicit model of good writing (and reading) holds enough range to be applied to any subject matter with little trouble. This results in language arts strategies and practices trumping the subject matters in which they are exercised. I am arguing that, especially in the later grades (5–12), this gets it backward. Good reading and language arts practices are *vehicles* for helping to generate deeper understandings in history (or earth science, mathematics, or economics), not ends in themselves. Therefore, the learning model specific to historical thinking and understanding must define what good reading and writing look like in that domain, rather than the other way around. Without this shift, historical understanding suffers.

Aligning assessment tasks and interpretive rubrics to teaching practices and classroom activities is fundamentally about learning models. Without clear models that are subject-domain specific, it is difficult to attain adequate connections between points on the assessment triangle. Consequently, it becomes increasingly difficult to say much about growth in domain cognition and understanding. The standards documents, despite all their rhetoric about improving thinking and understanding, lack for explicit articulations of such learning models, especially ones that are domain specific. Therefore, it should be of little surprise that reading and language arts indicators are overapplied.

The authors of the ELA Common Core appeared to understand something about this set of issues. Disciplinary literacies (i.e., subject-specific reading and writing) seem to play a much larger role in the Common Core Standards than in previous standards efforts. However, the ELA Common Core does not explicitly identify the learning model within subjects such as history, from which it draws in order to identify its indicators. The social studies inquiry framework, although aligned to elements of the ELA Common Core, likewise does relatively little to clearly articulate a history-specific learning model and the progressions of learning that would underlie its developmental trajectory. Without articulated and detailed subject-specific learning models, it is anyone's guess what assessment practices and interpretive rubrics will look like that emerge in states that elect to adopt the standards and framework.

What I have attempted to do in the preceding chapters is to begin filling in this blank, to sketch out how a history-specific learning model can shape assessment tasks and interpretive rubrics. In doing so, I am trying to map a route toward providing teachers and students with the diagnostic feedback necessary to help improve thinking and understanding in the subject domain of history.

Asking the question "Alignment to what?" ends up being a critical move. Although research on learning in subject domains is an ongoing endeavor, and one that will continue to reshape learning models, that research is rich enough to enable articulations of learning progressions that offer opportunities to align elements of the assessment triangle. In mathematics and science alone, the research-based models are robust enough that the editors and author team of *Knowing What Students Know* were able to provide ample illustrations of aligned, subject-specific assessment and interpretation strategies in science and mathematics. Yet strikingly absent from that volume were aligned assessment illustrations from the field of social studies education. That brings us to the question: How applicable might the history assessment ideas found in this book be to other social studies subjects such as economics, civics/government, and geography?

Are the Assessment Ideas in History Applicable to Other Subjects?

The short answer to this question is the equivocal yes and no. The almost immediate and self-evident no: All these school subjects derive from different disciplines animated by different questions and inquiry practices. It is probably no accident that there are no assessment examples in *Knowing What Students Know* for the domains of civics/government, economics, and geography, other important social education subjects taught in schools. Unlike the science and mathematics domains, and history to a large extent, research on learning in these three social studies subjects lags behind.[10] The result is that it is difficult to construct and articulate with any precision the learning models and progressions necessary to sufficiently align the three points of the assessment triangle.

We do understand some things about what children and adolescents know in these three fields, and efforts have been made to clarify learning targets.[11] But the progressions in learning from the novice level to that of competence remain rather murky. Also, and unlike in history, we lack the clear exemplars for what expertise looks like in doing geography or doing economics, for example. Without that expertise research, it is difficult to establish research-defensible learning targets, and so therefore troublesome to identify the steps in progression toward expert understanding. As a result, it can be challenging to create sound assessment tasks and interpretive rubrics that will provide diagnostic power for teachers. A weak or incomplete learning model tends to produce weak, incomplete, or domain-distorted outcome data and impoverished interpretations of what those data mean. This is the space in which generic reading and writing rubrics frequently get confused with and/or substituted for domain-specific ones, and where domain cognition and understanding are sacrificed in the interests of being able to find the main idea in a paragraph.

Despite these problems, many of the principles inherent in the history education assessment tasks and rubrics I have sketched should allow for some transfer to these other social education domains. Achieving alignment between a research-based learning model, assessment tasks, and interpretation strategies would be one example. Designing tasks that allow for assessing a variety of different attributes of the learning model would be another. Applying a third principle would involve being sure to create tasks that not only sampled endpoint understandings, but also the thinking activities (e.g., reading, writing, analyzing, graphing, calculating) that are crucial to enabling that understanding. Yet what will make these principles tricky to apply in the civics/ government, economics, and geography domains is the absence of the requisite progression-oriented learning models. We need more systematic research on learning trajectories in these subject fields in order to construct adequate learning models, especially research on expertise.

The lack of research may create some difficulties for states that adopt the ELA Common Core and social studies inquiry framework. The ELA is generally silent about reading, writing, and thinking in these three pivotal social education fields. Even though the ELA contains only an implicit learning model for history education, the model does seem to be derived from research in that domain's specific forms of practice. It, therefore, does provide some sense of progression markers across its breadth and thus some guidance about teaching, learning, and assessment trajectories in history. The silence on literacy targets in civics/government, economics, and geography results in no guidance at all.

By contrast, the social studies inquiry framework makes these three domains (along with history) a central part of its inquiry-based instructional arc (question formulating→inquiry-space strategizing→ obtaining evidence to address questions→communicating results) and related learning indicators. Yet without clear learning models in civics/government, economics, and geography that contain progression markers rooted in domain-specific learning research, it remains to be seen how diagnostic assessments can be constructed that provide teachers and students with learning feedback. Short of additional learning research in those three fields, it is possible that alignment between the social education indicators and the assessments that measure attainment of them could be only partial, and thereby produce misaligned and distorted results.

Perhaps several intrepid researchers with broad knowledge of research work in those domains will take it upon themselves to cobble together the empirical studies on learning we do possess and shape it into at least the semblance of learning models with progression markers. Those domain-specific models could then be used to connect up the other two points of the assessment triangle.

Can These History Assessment Strategies Be Used in Large-scale Testing?

Again, I am pressed to equivocate. On the one hand, current large-scale, high-stakes testing practices adhere to a set of attitudes, values, and practices that are at odds with what I have been advocating: diagnostic, performance assessments that benefit teachers and learners most directly. Large-scale accountability testing works from principles that are primarily designed to evaluate programs in order to sort, select, and stratify test-takers. Ostensibly, they function to identify and separate out the "good" schools, teachers, and students from the "bad" ones. The good ones, then, get more resources and the bad ones are reconstituted or closed down. The principle is based on the neoliberal idea that such moves create more competition, and more competition for resources will make all schools better. Let the market rule. Yet that system seems at least implicitly cynical in that the accountability regime appears designed to suggest that there is something quite wrong with the teachers in the bad schools and action must be taken to stop them.

As a system of practices, high-stakes testing as an accountability approach appears to miss the point that schools (and the teachers and students that inhabit them) at least in the United States, are social institutions already embedded in a market economy and political culture, one that metes out rewards in a deeply uneven way. The result is a profoundly stratified society with perennially vast differences between those with extensive capital and those with little, between businesses that produce good products and those that produce lousy ones.[12] Why would we wonder if school systems did not also reflect that same type of stratification, especially since school funding in many places also operates on similar inequitable formulas?[13] If we cannot fully eliminate private marketplace woes, why would we imagine that the public marketplace would be any different?

The system and its advocates also seem to miss the point I referenced earlier that, if you wish to improve teaching and learning, you have to attend to teaching and learning.[14] High-stakes testing and program evaluation that operate externally, from outside classroom spaces, have not been shown to leverage significant change in helping students learn to think and understand subjects more deeply. Assessments designed and used within classrooms and by teachers and students have been shown to operate in precisely the opposite direction. It's the difference between testing as accountability and assessment as learning. The former may have certain legitimate purposes, but the latter has considerably more power for improving on teaching and learning.

There are other complications. When the stakes indeed are high, it comes as no surprise that testmakers and psychometricians become obsessed with test reliability issues rather than concerns about construct validity rooted in subject domains, as I noted in Chapter 1. To levy some form of legitimized sanctions on bad schools and bad teachers, policymakers and enforcers need reliable data on which to base those sanctions. As long as decisions can be carried out through testing practices that can meet the reliability standard, construct validity only demands some general lip service. If such tests are carefully guarded so that ostensibly they cannot be gamed, the secrecy makes it difficult to establish in real time what ideas, concepts, and understandings the tests are actually measuring. That secrecy also helps to allay testing agents' anxieties about validity concerns. But it does very little to assist teachers and students in improving teaching and learning.

It is true that tests items are released from time to time. Frequently, however, only a small number of items become visible. This makes it difficult to establish a reasonable sense of the validity of any test, say in history, as a whole and contemporaneously. These features of large-scale testing reveal that the attitudes and values that sit behind the practice are designed to achieve very different outcomes than what I have been suggesting. It is difficult to square up those two contrasting sets of attitudes and values. In that sense, the assessment strategies and interpretive rubrics you found in the foregoing chapters would seem hardly applicable to these high-stakes, large-scale testing and accountability schemes.

In effect, what I have been arguing for is a completely different definition of educational accountability.[15] I am seeking to define it where I think it matters the most, in the classroom and in the relationships among teachers, learners, and the subjects a learner is trying to understand. So I use the vocabulary of diagnostics rather than accountability to reframe the discussion. In order for diagnostic assessment to operate in a large-scale testing culture, that culture in many different ways would need to redefine its attitudes and values regarding the purposes for assessing. That is no small undertaking and, unfortunately, I do not see such a change occurring quickly.

Nevertheless, this rather dour perspective is far from definitive. To illustrate, I offer a brief anecdote that reveals how attitudes and values can begin to shift in a large, diverse public school system driven by a decades-old, high-stakes accountability culture. It is from experiences like this that I draw some hope from the depths of the cynicism that arises from the effect of defining accountability the way we currently seem obsessed with doing in the United States.

Over the course of the 10-year federal funding cycle of the Teaching American History grant program, this particular Maryland public school system received three 3-year grants. Effectively, history teachers in the system were funded almost continuously for a decade. My research/evaluation team and I served as program evaluators on the latter two of those grants and I worked as a history-education professional developer on the first iteration. Many of the assessment ideas and strategies you find on these pages were rigorously tested initially in the context of these TAH program evaluations. We wrote them for and used them with the history teachers in the program to obtain data about changes in their historical thinking and understanding across the programs' durations.

Although our charge was external, independent program evaluation, we worked hard to draw from principles of good assessment design that gauged participant learning and understanding. Our goal was to construct assessments that (a) were tied to the program's design and practices, (b) drew from a domain-specific learning model in history education, (c) aligned performances and interpretive rubrics to the learning model, and (d) produced diagnostic data that would be directly useful to program directors, planners, partners, and teachers. In this sense, we tried to marry two sets of practices with opposing attitudes and values—external program evaluation with diagnostic assessment.

Being a head program evaluator can be a delicate task. Sometimes you find yourself using the data you collect to tell program directors and professional development partners things they would rather not hear—for example, that certain aspects of the program designed to grow teachers' understanding are not working very well. What I found quite remarkable about this particular program was that the program director, who was also the social studies school system coordinator, actually listened to what the evaluation data were saying. He was particularly interested in how we went about gathering those data, and most importantly asked many questions about the construct validity of the assessment items we used, items much like the ones I have already described.

Near the end of the first of the two 3-year grants that we assessed and evaluated, the program director became convinced that the data we were gathering were indeed valid assessments of his teachers' learning growth and understanding (or the lack thereof). The primary goal of that program had been to shift teachers' ideas about teaching American history away from a simple coverage model that involved much teacher talk, and toward having teachers immerse their students in an investigation of the American past that cohered with the learning model described in Chapter 2.

Our assessment data revealed that teachers made progress in that regard but encountered two rather significant and interrelated obstacles. The first was that the teachers struggled to understand how to conceptualize the ingredients and flow necessary to sustain an actual historical investigation in the classroom and with their students. They needed clearer models and exemplars. The second obstacle followed from the first: The school system's extant American history curriculum stressed rapid coverage of a bloated array of topics and periods followed by district-level end-of-quarter tests that reinforced coverage. Teachers had discovered early on that investigations take more time to teach than brisk coverage approaches. They were anxious about the unit tests and about covering the breadth of the curriculum sufficiently. Those worries repeatedly derailed their efforts to mount the sustained investigations they were learning about in the program.

As the project director and partners began to write their third TAH grant, they used the assessment results to make three changes. First, the project director pushed through a curricular shift that would exempt the next group of TAH teacher participants from coverage pressures. Second, the new grant would make the investigations procedures and flow much more explicit to participants, going so far as to develop a step-by-step template of how to accomplish one, followed by guided practice in building and then actually teaching them. And third, in order to assess whether such investigations, and the student learning model from which they drew, improved student thinking and understanding in history, the project director sought to design and apply student versions of the weighted multiple-choice items (WMCs) modeled on the ones we were using in our assessment approach. The project director hired three history teachers to work with our evaluation team to write the WMCs.

The intention was to administer these WMCs along with DBQ-type essay questions (see Chapter 3) to large numbers of students in the school system. The design was quasi-experimental. There were to be approximately 15 schools in which participating teachers would teach their investigative units. Over 1,000 students would be affected by the teaching of those units across the 15 schools. With some guidance from us, the project director identified 15 other schools and history teachers who would not be participating in the third TAH program. Those schools were to be as closely paired as possible on overall SES data, reading test scores, geographic location, school size, and student grade level. The history students in the latter cluster of schools would eventually serve as a comparison group for the students in the TAH schools in a quasi-experimental assessment design.

We met with the three history-teacher assessment writers periodically during the first 12 months of the now-funded third TAH grant. Our sessions were designed to teach the teachers how to write WMCs based on the principles I have outlined. We then worked with them to check item validity, edit, clarify, and otherwise hone these WMCs (and later essay tasks) into ones that could be administered to respective groups of fifth, eighth, and ninth graders. The first administration of this new assessment to over 2,000 students occurred late in that school year, approximately 1,000 each from the experimental and comparison classrooms.

Working with district testing personnel, the project director developed a method of running the WMCs through a Scantron four times (students had used bubble sheets for the WMCs), once each to identify how many 4-point responses were chosen, then again for how many 2-point responses, and so on. The data displays that followed from this process allowed the project director to assess how well the teachers affected by the TAH program fared relative to the comparison school teachers on growing student thinking and understanding in history. This served as a method for providing him diagnostic information about the success of the TAH program. The next step involved also teaching other teachers how to design such assessments for regular in-class use. At last report, the project director was working to use this type of assessment approach to replace the end-of-quarter, traditional multiple-choice tests that had been common practice for many years.

My point in narrating this account is to observe how, with some dedicated internal effort and, of course, some external investment, at least one small corner of a school system can begin to reshape itself, to move away from what I'm calling a testing-culture approach and toward a classroom assessment-culture model. Returning to my earlier equivocation, I want to observe that applying the approach I am advocating to uses beyond individual classroom contexts can be possible. That this possibility exists might make it more than worth the trouble. However, its promise can only be fully realized if that broader, say, school-wide use, translates into fundamental support for a diagnostic assessment approach carried out by teachers in those individual classrooms. As before, basing the approach on and rooting it within a learning model—from lone classroom to school system writ large—becomes crucial to the overall efficacy of making the shift. Again, it is all about alignment.

What About the Cost?

In the foregoing account there are references to issues of expense. It is reasonable to ask what such a diagnostic assessment approach costs and how does it get paid for and by whom. Clearly, such a system looks expensive. But there are a number of different ways to think about cost, and not all of them should necessarily make educational accountants, superintendents, and policymakers cringe. Here I take up this issue briefly with full acknowledgement that I am far from an expert in actuarial analyses or asset-liability comparisons. Because of this, I wish to talk less about monetary costs and more about educational costs—*and* benefits. Actually, it might be better to say that I will be discussing opportunity costs more than anything else.

High-stakes accountability and testing systems are very expensive. Few would deny that. Every year vast sums of money flow out of public schools into the private sector as school systems buy costly testing products from large, private corporations that have built a cottage industry around the accountability movement legislated by the *No Child Left Behind* federal law. Arguably, one could make a reasonable case that this transfer of payments from public to private sector is a form of mass corporate subsidizing, precipitated by local and state governments all across the United States and driven by legal mandate. Some might even call it a brand of corporate welfare.

What does the public get in exchange for this vast transfer of payments? From an educational perspective, the evidence is mounting that it receives very little. We have known for decades, long before the advent of external, high-stakes testing as a form of accountability, that educational poverty follows from personal poverty. The current high-stakes testing efforts only reinforce our comprehension of that long-understood problem. Yes, the high-stakes testing system does call even more attention to the issue of poverty (educational and personal). But mass testing as a fix-it strategy tends to strip resources away from school systems efforts to address it because so many of those resources leave the system and move into the private sector. Public schools end up facing many sticks with very few carrots left to enact real change. Punishment for poor performance alone is not enough.[16]

A number of scholars have been maintaining for some time that the opportunity cost of investing so heavily in external testing-as-accountability systems is not worth bearing. Diagnostic, performance assessment systems, carefully aligned to powerful learning models, designed and built by and for teachers, used regularly in classrooms to focus on and improve learning, show the best hope for bringing about educational change and reform. More rigorous standards alone, even if they are tied to strong learning models, also are not enough without investments in growing teachers' understanding of how to work with them. What the mounting evidence appears to be telling us is that unless we divest ourselves of the idea that external testing-as-accountability systems will fix things and train more attention on and invest more heavily in teaching and learning practices at the classroom level, the cost will only be more educational poverty.

It is also expensive to educate teachers both before they enter the profession and certainly once they are there. Building diagnostic assessment systems with and for teachers and helping them learn how to successfully apply them would be one part of this expense. Aligning standards and indicators with robust learning models, such as the one I have described and similar versions in science and mathematics, would be another. But these efforts are focused on teaching-and-learning improvements and situated where both matter the most, at the classroom level.

In the zero-sum game of public education finance, resources must be transferred from one arena to another to make headway. What scholars and policy analysts of the public school systems have been arguing, if I read them correctly, is that the transfer must involve slowing private-sector resource outflow, retaining those funds, and investing them internally, in teacher professional development. The assessment approach I have described is one place in which to reinvest those resources if the conversation is to become increasingly about educational richness for *all students*, rather than the educational poverty of some.

★ ★ ★ ★ ★

At the risk of belaboring the point, I want to stress again that, at least in the case of history education, I have been attempting to chart a path toward this type of teacher-focused, classroom-embedded, learning-attentive assessment practice. To follow that path requires a shift in attitudes toward what matters and how to successfully address what matters. I am arguing that the path leads to the classroom, to a place where some very important learning activities can occur. The principal actors in that effort are teachers and students. Without direct, internal attention to those activities and interchanges and the people who engage in them there, we will find ourselves in a decade or two still wringing our hands about what to do to fix matters, all while a constructive path still points the way forward.

On the Hope of Educational Opulence

In this short volume, I have tried to contribute to a larger conversation about how to improve education, and specifically one small element of it called history education. As I have also attempted to show, particularly in this last chapter, the ideas, models, approaches, and examples all require careful alignment if the assessment approach I am proposing will be beneficial to teachers and their students. However, I am under no illusion that accomplishing this will be easy or simple work.

States and school systems will need to embrace a learning model in history education that has been largely foreign to their common coverage-dominated, nation-state narrative approaches. They will need the expertise and resources to work with history teachers to help them understand the learning model, and the pedagogical practices it entails, in order to realize its benefits for student learning. Performative, diagnostic assessments aligned with the model will need to be constructed and their applications supported. Powerful interpretive rubrics will have to follow. The data the assessments generate and what they say about and do for student learning will need to be trusted and valued within systems. For their part, history teachers will need to acquire a spirit of openness to the possibilities these changes can create. They in turn will need to persuade their students of those benefits. Effectively the culture will need to shift away from testing, grading, sorting, and selecting and toward learning and understanding—for all students.

This is a tall order. But as I have attempted to demonstrate, it is worth the effort and it is supported by decades of research work. The path leads out of the despair of chronic reports of educational poverty and toward a more hopeful conversation about educational opulence, for history education at the very least.

Notes

1 See http://www.achieve.org and http://www.smarterbalanced.org. For arguments by scholars and researchers, see for example, http://www.cshc. ubc.ca/projects/#assessing_historical and http://beyondthebubble.stanford. edu.

2 See, for example, the case made by Achieve at http://www.achieve.org.

3 The quote is from the EdSteps website (www.edsteps.org).

4 See http://www.ccsso.org/Documents/2012/11%2012%2012%20Vision%20 Statement%20College%20Career%20and%20Civic%20Life%20Frame work.pdf.

5 There are any number of countervailing pressures and circumstances that can prevent such shifts from occurring. Typical 19th- and 20th-century conceptions of learning and the role knowledge acquisition plays in those conceptions are not well aligned to the newer conceptions. Entrenched organizational structures in education also resist change. And the current stress on leveraging educational change through legally mandated accountability and external testing generally do little to support efforts to

reconceptualize learning goals. All present formidable challenges to the more recent vocabulary of reform in educational assessment and learning.

6 One of the most impressive, evidence-backed cases for the importance of classroom-based diagnostic assessments has been made by Black and Wiliam. See Paul Black and Dylan Wiliam, "Assessment and Classroom Learning," *Assessment in Education, 5* (1998), pp. 7–73. See also Carlos Ayala, Richard Shavelson, Maria Areceli Ruiz-Primo, Paul Brandon, Yue Yin, Erin Marie Furtak, and Donald Young, "From Formal Embedded Assessments to Reflective Lessons: The Development of Formative Assessment Studies," *Applied Measurement in Education, 21* (2008), pp. 315–334.

7 Chauncey Monte-Sano, "What Makes a Good Historical Essay? Assessing Historical Aspects of Argumentative Writing," *Social Education, 76* (November/December 2012), pp. 294–298. The quote is taken from page 294.

8 Pellegrino et al., *Knowing What Students Know.*

9 See, for example, Susan S. Stodolsky, *The Subject Matters: Classroom Activity in Math and Social Studies* (Chicago: University of Chicago Press, 1988); Lee S. Shulman, *The Wisdom of Practice: Essays on Teaching, Learning, and Learning to Teach* (San Francisco: Jossey-Bass, 2004), especially Chapter 15; Bruce VanSledright, *In Search of America's Past: Learning to Read History in Elementary School* (New York: Teachers College Press, 2002); and Sam Wineburg, *Historical Thinking and Other Unnatural Acts: Charting the Future of Teaching the Past* (Philadelphia: Temple University Press, 2001), especially Chapters 6–8.

10 Steven Miller and Phillip VanFossen, "Recent Research on the Teaching and Learning of Pre-Collegiate Economics," in Linda Levstik and Cynthia Tyson (Eds.), *Handbook of Research in Social Studies Education* (New York: Routledge, 2008), pp. 284–304; Avner Segall and Robert Helfenbein, "Research on K-12 Geography Education," in Linda Levstik and Cynthia Tyson (Eds.), *Handbook of Research in Social Studies Education* (New York: Routledge, 2008), pp. 259–283; and Bruce VanSledright and Margarita Limon, "Learning and Teaching in Social Studies: Cognitive Research on History and Geography," in Patricia Alexander and Philip Winne (Eds.), *The Handbook of Educational Psychology, 2nd Ed.* (Mahwah, NJ: Lawrence Erlbaum Associates), pp. 545–570.

11 See Miller and VanFossen, "Recent Research;" Segall and Helfenbein, "Research on K-12 Geography" and Robert Hess and Judith Torney, *The Development of Political Attitudes in Children* (Piscataway, NJ: Transaction Publishers, 1967/2009).

12 Critics will be quick to note that the marketplace weeds out those who produce poor products. This may be the case, but new ones spring up in

their place overnight. As the ancient proverb duly notes, poverty will be with you always, including marketplace poverty. Think credit-swap derivatives and sub-prime mortgages.

13 See, for example, Jonathan Kozol's *Shame of the Nation: The Return of Aparthied Schooling in America* (New York: Broadway, 2006), and *Savage Inequalities: Children in America's Schools* (New York: Harper, 1992).
14 David Cohen and Susan Moffitt, *The Ordeal of Equality*.
15 I am hardly the first to make this case. See note 6.
16 David K. Cohen, Susan L. Moffitt, and Simona Goldin, "Policy and Practice: The Dilemma," *American Journal of Education, 113* (2007), pp. 515–548.

Appendix

ADDITIONAL WEIGHTED MULTIPLE-CHOICE ITEMS AND SCORING STRUCTURES

The following items are presented here to demonstrate a range of possible historical topics and substantive (first-order) ideas that can be assessed through WMC items. These five items sample ideas spanning early European explorations of North America through the Cold War period. The items' scoring structures proceed from the same principles and theories outlined in Chapter 4. Using such items with students younger than high school age would require language and word modifications to make them more accessible and reader friendly.

Currently, the most reasonable research-based hypothesis for explaining the quick decline of the native population in Central America between 1520 and 1600 is

   a. Global climate changes which impacted food production

   b. The arrival and spread of contagious European diseases

   c. A system that forced natives to labor for Spanish settlers

   d. The superior weapons technology of the conquistadors

4-point option = b. 2-point option = d. 1-point option = c. 0-point option = a.

Consult: Russell Thornton, *American Indian Holocaust and Survival: A Population History Since 1492* (Norman, OK: University of Oklahoma Press, 1990).

Research on Lewis and Clark's western expedition to explore and chart the United States' Louisiana Purchase suggests that that expedition

    a. Had limited long-term consequences for the development of the United States

    b. Was considered one of the most successful scientific expeditions in U.S. history

    c. Signaled the forthcoming decline of Native American culture in North America

    d. Worsened United States government and Native American relations at the time

4-point option = c. 2-point option = b. 1-point option = d. 0-point option = a.

Consult: Laurie Winn Carlson, *Seduced by the American West: Jefferson's America and the Lure of the Land Beyond the Mississippi* (Chicago: Ivan R. Dee Publishers, 2003) and James P. Ronda, *Lewis and Clark Among the Indians* (Lincoln, NE: University of Nebraska Press, 2002).

Recent historical evidence relating to slave resistance in America suggests that

    a. Many slaves were satisfied with their existence

    b. Open rebellions in plantation communities did occur

    c. Subtle forms of opposition often went unnoticed

    d. As many as 50,000 slaves ran away each year

4-point option = c. 2-point option = d. 1-point option = b. 0-point option = a.

Consult: James H. Sweet, "Slave Resistance." Available online at: http://national humanitiescenter.org/tserve/freedom/1609–1865/essays/slaveresist.htm.

Recent revised cultural histories argue that the arrival of different immigrant groups throughout the development of the United States has led to

    a. The creation of a vibrant American melting pot

    b. A continuous redefinition of national identity

    c. A renewed belief in a pure American culture

    d. The enrichment of cultural diversity and pluralism

4-point option = b. 2-point option = d. 1-point option = c. 0-point option = c.

Consult: Gary Gerstle and John Mollenkopf (Eds.), *E Pluribus Unum: Contemporary and Historical Perspectives on Immigrant Political Incorporation* (New York: Russell Sage, 2001).

Although disagreements exist among Cold War analysts, they do agree on which of the following statements about the Iron Curtain? It was

a. A term describing the wall dividing East from West Berlin

b. A term attributed to Stalin's strategy to consume much of Eastern Europe

c. An imaginary line separating a democratic West and a communist East

d. An idea forwarded by Churchill referring to containment of the Soviets

4-point option = c. 2-point option = a. 1-point option = d. 0-point option = b.

Consult: Anne Applebaum, *Iron Curtain: The Crushing of Eastern Europe, 1944–1956* (New York: Doubleday, 2012).

INDEX

Note: Page numbers in *italics* indicate figures.